Cash and Financial Management

Workbook

Aubrey Penning

Published by Osborne Books Limited
Tel 01905 748071
Email books@osbornebooks.co.uk
Website www.osbornebooks.co.uk

Design by Laura Ingham

British Library Cataloguing in Publication Data
A catalogue record for this book is available from the British Library

ISBN 978-1-911198-81-9

Contents

Introduction

Chapter activities

Answers to chapter activities

Practice assessments

Answers to practice assessments

Introduction

Qualifications covered

This book has been written specifically to cover the Unit 'Cash and Financial Management' which is optional for the following qualifications:

AAT Level 4 Diploma in Professional Accounting

AAT Diploma in Professional Accounting – SCQF Level 8

This book contains Chapter Activities which provide extra practice material in addition to the activities included in the Osborne Books Tutorial text, and Practice Assessments to prepare the student for the computer based assessments. The latter are based directly on the structure, style and content of the sample assessment material provided by the AAT at www.aat.org.uk.

Suggested answers to the Chapter Activities and Practice Assessments are set out in this book.

Osborne Study and Revision Materials

Additional materials, tailored to the needs of students studying this unit and revising for the assessment, include:

- **Tutorials:** paperback books with practice activities
- **Student Zone:** access to Osborne Books online resources
- **Osborne Books App:** Osborne Books ebooks for mobiles and tablets

Visit www.osbornebooks.co.uk for details of study and revision resources and access to online material.

Chapter activities

1 Managing cash flows

1.1

(a)   Complete the diagram below of the working capital cycle by placing the options into the correct boxes.

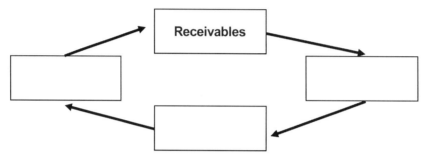

Options:

- Payables
- Cash
- Inventory

(b)   A business has an average inventory holding period of 95 days, receives payment from its customers in 55 days and pays its suppliers in 80 days.

What is the cash operating cycle in days for the business? (Select **one** option).

(a)	230 days	
(b)	120 days	
(c)	40 days	
(d)	70 days	

1.2   Complete the following table by selecting one or more appropriate phrases for each box from the options listed.

Term	Meaning	Signs Include
Overtrading		
Overcapitalisation		

Options for **'Meaning'**:

- Too much working capital

- Too little working capital

- The right amount of working capital

Options for **'Signs Include'**:

- Rapidly increasing sales volumes

- Reduced value of trade receivables

- High cash balances

- Payments made to suppliers before they are due

- Overdrawn bank balances

- Payments made late to suppliers

- Increased profit margins

1.3 Identify and tick the correct statements from those listed in the table below.

(a)	Receipts that relate to the proceeds from the disposal of non-current assets are capital receipts	
(b)	Payments that relate to the acquisition of non-current assets are regular revenue payments	
(c)	Payments made to the owners of the business are capital receipts	
(d)	Income received from the operating activities of the business that is expected to occur frequently is a regular revenue receipt	
(e)	Income received from the operating activities of the business that is not expected to occur frequently is a regular revenue receipt	
(f)	Payments arising from the operating activities of the business that are expected to occur frequently are regular revenue payments	
(g)	Payments that relate to the acquisition of non-current assets are capital payments	
(h)	The receipt of a bank loan is an example of an exceptional receipt	

1.4 A business currently has the following features:

- sales are increasing, leading to increased trade receivables
- inventory is being increased to satisfy increased demand
- payments to suppliers are being delayed due to a shortage of cash

Is the business likely to be experiencing:

(a)	Overcapitalisation?	
(b)	Normal trading?	
(c)	Overtrading?	
(d)	Stagnation?	

Tick the **one** correct option

1.5 Complete the following table by ticking the appropriate column to indicate the category of each payment example.

Example	Capital payment	Regular revenue payment	Payment for drawings	Exceptional payment
Dividends				
Acquisition of new business				
Purchase of raw materials				
Purchase of computer				
Payment of Corporation Tax				
Repayment of whole loan				

2 Forecasting data for cash budgets

2.1 Freddo Limited is preparing its forecast sales and purchase information for January of next year.

The sales volume trend is to be identified using a 3-point moving average based on the actual monthly sales volumes for the current year.

(a) Complete the table below to calculate the monthly sales volume trend and identify any monthly variations

	Sales volume (units)	Trend	Monthly variation (volume less trend)
August	56,160		
September	35,640		
October	31,320		
November	59,400		
December	38,880		

The monthly sales volume trend is [   ] units.

Additional information:

- The selling price per unit has been set at £5.

- Monthly purchases are estimated to be 60% of the value of the forecast sales.

- The seasonal variations operate on a three month repeating cycle.

(b) Using the trend and the monthly variations identified in part (a), complete the table below to forecast the sales volume, sales value and purchase value for January of the next financial year.

	Forecast trend	Variation	Forecast sales volume	Forecast sales £	Forecast purchases £
January					

2.2 A company has a forecast cost of £195.00 for a new product that it will manufacture. Complete the following table to show the range of forecast selling prices and gross profits.

Round each selling price to the nearest penny.

	Selling Price £.p	**Gross Profit** £.p
Mark-up of 10%		
Mark-up of 15%		
Margin of 15%		
Margin of 20%		

2.3 A computer program has used linear regression to analyse the sales data of a swimwear manufacturer. Using quarter numbers (quarter 35 is the first quarter of year 20-1), the sales trend has been determined as:

Sales Trend (in £) = (Quarter Number x £550) + £78,500.

The Seasonal Variations have been determined as the following percentages of the trend:

Quarter 1	−12%
Quarter 2	+55%
Quarter 3	+15%
Quarter 4	−58%

Required:

Use the above data to calculate the forecast of sales in £ for each quarter of 20-3.

2.4 The cost of an electronic component has been falling by an average of 2% every six months. In January 20-5 the cost of the component is £50. Assuming the cost continues to behave in the same way in the future, what is the forecast cost in July 20-6?

(a)	£47.00	
(b)	£48.00	
(c)	£48.02	
(d)	£47.06	

2.5   Chocco Limited is forecasting the cost of a certain type of cocoa, which is one of the raw materials for its chocolate products. The cost was £1,890 per tonne in April 20-1. The following index data (actual and forecast) is available:

	Consumer Price Index	**Raw Cocoa Price Index**
April 20-1 Actual	471	163
April 20-2 Forecast	485	194

Using the most appropriate data, forecast the cost per tonne of cocoa in April 20-2 to the nearest £.

£ [   ]

2.6   The following historical data relates to sales in units.

	Quarter 1	**Quarter 2**	**Quarter 3**	**Quarter 4**
Year 10	4,000	3,440	2,640	2,240
Year 11	3,680	3,120	2,320	1,920
Year 12	3,360	2,800	2,000	1,600
Year 13	3,040	2,480	1,680	1,280

Required:

(a)   Using centred moving averages, analyse this data into the trend and additive seasonal variations.

Quarter	Sales units	4-point averages	Centred averages (trend)	Seasonal variations
Y10 Q1				
Q2				
Q3				
Q4				
Y11 Q1				
Q2				
Q3				
Q4				
Y12 Q1				
Q2				
Q3				
Q4				
Y13 Q1				
Q2				
Q3				
Q4				

(b)   Use the data to forecast the unit sales for each quarter of year 14.

Year 14	Forecast trend	Seasonal variations	Forecast
Q1			
Q2			
Q3			
Q4			

2.7   The following historical data has been extracted from company records. The data relates to the purchase price per kilogram of a raw material.

Month	Jan	Feb	March	April	May	June
Price £	200.30	201.35	200.95	201.80	203.50	203.65
Index						

Required:

Create an index based on these prices, using January as the base point. Calculate your index numbers to two decimal places.

3 Preparing cash budgets

3.1 Martha owns a greengrocer's shop and prepares annual income statements and statements of financial position. These are prepared on an accruals basis.

Since the fruit and vegetables that she sells are perishable, no inventory is held at the year-end (when the business is closed over the holiday period). Some sales are made on a cash basis and some on a credit basis. All purchases are made on credit terms.

The income statement for Martha's business for the year ended 31 December 20-5 is as follows:

	£	£
Sales		128,900
Less: Purchases		(50,060)
Gross profit		78,840
Less: Expenses		
Wages	21,400	
Rent of shop	12,000	
Shop expenses	5,350	
Depreciation of shop fittings	500	
Bank charges	350	
		39,600
		39,240

During 20-5, Martha took £20,000 from the business in drawings.

Extracts from the statements of financial position at 31 December 20-4 and 31 December 20-5 show the following:

Statement of financial position at	31 Dec 20-4	31 Dec 20-5
	£	£
Trade Receivables	1,200	1,840
Trade Payables	8,900	7,630
Accruals – shop expenses	190	210
Accruals – bank charges	0	50
Prepayments – rent of shop	1,200	1,500

(a) Calculate the actual business cash receipts and cash payments for the year to 31 December 20-5.

	£
Sales receipts	
Purchases payments	
Wages paid	
Rent paid	
Shop expenses	
Depreciation	
Bank charges	
Drawings	
Net cash flow	

(b) Use the following table to reconcile the profit with the net cash flow (from part (a)). Use minus signs for amounts to be deducted.

	£
Profit	39,240
Change in trade receivables	
Change in trade payables	
Change in accruals	
Change in prepayments	
Adjustment for non-cash expenditure	
Drawings paid	
Net cash flow	

3.2   The cash budget for Haven Industries for the three months ended June has been partially completed. The following information is to be incorporated and the cash budget completed.

- A bank loan of £52,800 has been negotiated and this will be paid into the business bank account in April.

- The principal (capital) element of the bank loan (£52,800) is to be repaid in 48 equal monthly instalments beginning in May.

- The loan attracts 12% interest per annum calculated on the amount of the loan principal advanced in April. The annual interest charge is to be paid in equal monthly instalments beginning in May.

- When Haven Industries uses its bank overdraft facility, interest is payable monthly and is estimated at 2% of the previous month's overdraft balance. The interest is to be rounded to the nearest £.

- At 1 April the balance of the bank account was £1,750.

Using the additional information above, complete the cash budget for Haven Industries for the three months ending June. Cash inflows should be entered as positive figures and cash outflows as negative figures. Zeros must be entered where appropriate to achieve full marks.

	April £	May £	June £
RECEIPTS			
Cash sales	8,800	9,180	10,480
Credit sales	53,085	53,520	64,852
Bank loan		0	0
Total receipts			
PAYMENTS			
Purchases	−36,650	−37,005	−42,075
Wages	−18,800	−18,950	−18,450
Expenses	−10,350	−11,260	−13,260
Capital expenditure	0	−59,500	0
Bank loan capital repayment	0		
Bank loan interest	0		
Overdraft interest	0		
Total payments			
Net cash flow			
Opening bank balance			
Closing bank balance			

3.3 Minor Enterprises Limited has been trading for a number of years. The business has requested assistance with calculating sales receipts for entry into a cash budget.

Actual sales values achieved are available for January and February, and forecast sales values have been produced for March to June.

Minor Enterprises Limited estimates that cash sales account for 30% of the total sales. The remaining 70% of sales are made on a credit basis.

(a) Complete the table below to show the split of total sales between cash sales and credit sales.

	Actual sales £		Forecast sales £			
	January	February	March	April	May	June
Total sales	18,500	19,600	19,100	22,000	21,600	23,400
Cash sales						
Credit sales						

(b) Minor Enterprises estimates that 60% of credit sales are received in the month after sale with the balance being received two months after sale. For example, 60% of January's credit sales are received in February with the balance being received in March.

Using the table below and your figures from part (a), calculate the timing of sales receipts from credit sales that would be included in a cash budget for Minor Enterprises Limited for the period March to June.

	Credit sales £		Cash received				
			February £	March £	April £	May £	June £
January							
February							
March							
April							
May							
Monthly credit sales receipts							

3.4 Bishopswood Ltd is preparing cash payment figures ready for inclusion in a cash budget. The following information is relevant to the payment patterns for purchases, wages and expenses.

- Purchases are calculated as 65% of the next month's forecast sales and are paid two months after the date of purchase. For example, purchases in July are based on the estimated sales for August and paid for in September.

	Actual			Forecast		
	July £	August £	September £	October £	November £	December £
Total sales	71,000	77,800	76,200	80,000	85,000	87,000

- Wages are paid in the month that they are incurred and expenses are paid in the month after they are incurred. The actual and forecast figures for wages and expenses are:

	Actual			Forecast		
	July £	August £	September £	October £	November £	December £
Wages	8,500	8,750	9,000	8,800	8,700	8,950
Expenses (excluding depreciation)	7,450	9,010	6,450	7,100	8,050	7,300

- A new machine is to be purchased in October at a total cost of £40,500. Payment for the machine is to be made in three equal monthly instalments, beginning in October.

- The machine is to be depreciated monthly on a straight-line basis at 20% per annum.

Prepare an extract of the payments section of the cash budget for Bishopswood Ltd for the three months ended December.

	October £	November £	December £
PAYMENTS			
Purchases			
Wages			
Expenses			
New machine			
Total payments			

3.5 Capital Limited has budgeted for the following levels of raw material inventory (in units) over the next few periods:

Inventory (in units) at start of following periods:

Period 1	Period 2	Period 3	Period 4	Period 5
1,070	1,200	1,375	1,080	1,500

The raw materials usage budget shows the following figures (in units) for the same periods:

Period 1	Period 2	Period 3	Period 4	Period 5
5,650	7,480	4,890	4,850	6,990

Each unit of raw material costs £40 to purchase.

Payments for purchases are made as follows from Period 1 onwards:

60% of raw material purchases are paid in the period after delivery

30% of raw material purchases are paid two periods after delivery

10% of raw material purchases are paid three periods after delivery

Required:

Calculate the amounts to be paid for raw materials in each of periods 3 and 4. You may use the following tables if you wish.

	Period 1 units	Period 2 units	Period 3 units	Period 4 units	Period 5 units
Raw materials usage					
– opening inventory					
+ closing inventory					
= raw materials purchases					

	Payments in Periods:				
	Total £	Period 2 £	Period 3 £	Period 4 £	Period 5 £
Period 1 purchases					
Period 2 purchases					
Period 3 purchases					
Total purchase payments					

4 Using cash budgets

4.1   A cash budget has been prepared for Knightswood Ltd for the next five periods.

The budget was prepared based on the following sales volumes and a selling price of £15 per item.

	Period 1	**Period 2**	**Period 3**	**Period 4**	**Period 5**
Sales volume (items)	4,200	4,100	4,400	4,500	4,600

The pattern of cash receipts used in the budget assumes 50% of sales will be received in the month of sale and the remaining 50% in the month following sale.

In the light of current economic trends, Knightswood Ltd needs to adjust its cash budget to take account of the following:

- The selling price from period 1 will be reduced by 10% per item.

- The pattern of sales receipts changes to 30% of sales received in the month of sale, 50% in the month following sale and the remaining 20% two months after sale.

(a)   Use the table below to calculate the effect of the changes in the forecast amounts and timing of cash receipts for periods 3, 4 and 5:

	Period 1 £	**Period 2 £**	**Period 3 £**	**Period 4 £**	**Period 5 £**
Original value of forecast sales	63,000	61,500	66,000	67,500	69,000
Original timing of receipts			63,750	66,750	68,250
Revised value of forecast sales					
Revised timing of receipts					

Additional information:

The company's suppliers have negotiated reduced payment terms with Knightswood Ltd in return for fixing prices in the medium term. The original budget was prepared on the basis of paying suppliers in the month following purchase. The revised payment terms allow for settlement of 20% in the month of purchase, with the remaining 80% payment in the month following purchase. These revised terms come into effect for purchases in period 3, and therefore the payments in period 3 will consist of 20% of that month's purchases, plus all the period 2 purchases.

The original budgeted purchase figures were:

	Period 1 £	Period 2 £	Period 3 £	Period 4 £	Period 5 £
Purchases	30,500	31,200	30,800	32,000	33,000

(b) Use the table below to calculate the effect of the changes in the timing of purchase payments for periods 3, 4 and 5:

	Period 3 £	Period 4 £	Period 5 £
Original timing of payments			
Revised timing of payments			

(c) Using your calculations from parts (a) and (b), complete the table to show the net effect of the changes to sales receipts and purchase payments for periods 3, 4 and 5.

	Period 3 £	Period 4 £	Period 5 £
Changes in sales receipts			
Changes in purchase payments			
Net change			

4.2   The quarterly budgeted and actual figures for an organisation are provided below:

	Budgeted	Actual
	£	£
Receipts from credit customers	95,340	93,260
Cash sales	20,150	15,400
Payments to credit suppliers	(54,900)	(63,150)
Cash purchases	(4,500)	(3,450)
Capital expenditure	(18,500)	–
Wages and salaries	(18,600)	(18,300)
General expenses	(28,500)	(31,464)
Net cash flow	(9,510)	(7,704)
Opening bank balance	14,200	14,200
Closing bank balance	4,690	6,496

Prepare a reconciliation of budgeted cash flow with actual cash flow for the quarter. Select the appropriate description for each entry, and show + or – signs to denote increased or reduced cash. Ensure that the reconciliation balances.

	£
Budgeted closing bank balance	
Surplus/Shortfall in receipts from credit customers	
Surplus/Shortfall in cash sales	
Increase/Decrease in payments to credit suppliers	
Increase/Decrease in cash purchases	
Increase/Decrease in capital expenditure	
Increase/Decrease in wages and salaries	
Increase/Decrease in general expenses	
Actual closing bank balance	

4.3 Variances between budgeted and actual cash flows can occur for a number of reasons. There are also a variety of courses of action available to minimise adverse variances or benefit from favourable variances.

Match each cause of a variance listed on the left with a possible course of action on the right.

Labour costs have increased	Improve credit control
Sales volumes have decreased	Ensure available credit is being taken
Payments to suppliers are being made earlier	Increase labour efficiency
Customers are taking more days to settle their debts	Change suppliers
Prices of raw materials have increased	Provide salespeople with incentives

4.4 A company has forecast the following sales of a new product that will commence sales in Month 1:

	Month 1 £	Month 2 £	Month 3 £	Month 4 £	Total £
Forecast Sales	183,500	198,000	206,800	210,400	798,700

The expected receipts from sales are that:

- 10% are received in the month of sale (cash sales)

- 30% are received in the month following the sale

- 60% are received two months following the sale

This has produced the following initial forecast of receipts:

	Receipts from Sales in:				
	Month 1 £	Month 2 £	Month 3 £	Month 4 £	Total £
Month 1 Sales	18,350	55,050	110,100		
Month 2 Sales		19,800	59,400	118,800	
Month 3 Sales			20,680	62,040	
Month 4 Sales				21,040	
Forecast Receipts	18,350	74,850	190,180	201,880	485,260

The company is now considering offering a discount of 5% for credit customers who pay in the month following sale. This is expected to change the receipts profile to the following:

- 10% of sales are received in the month of sale (cash sales)

- 60% of sales are received in the month following the sale

- 30% of sales are received two months following the sale

All solutions should be shown to the nearest £ where appropriate.

(a) Complete the following table to show the expected receipts if the settlement discount is offered.

	Receipts from Sales in:				
	Month 1 £	Month 2 £	Month 3 £	Month 4 £	Total £
Month 1 Sales					
Month 2 Sales					
Month 3 Sales					
Month 4 Sales					
Forecast Receipts					

(b) Calculate the increased or reduced receipts in months 1 to 4 by completing the following table and using + or − signs.

	Month 1 £	Month 2 £	Month 3 £	Month 4 £	Net Total £
Change in Cash Flow					

(c) Calculate the amount of discount that will be allowed on the sales made in months 1 to 4 based on the above assumptions.

5 The UK financial system and liquidity

5.1 The interbank market is a money market where:

(a)	Bank customers pay large sums of money to each other using the banking system	
(b)	Banks make short-term loans to each other	
(c)	Money brokers trade bank shares with each other on behalf of clients	

Select the **one** correct option.

5.2 Open Market Operations (OMOs) can involve:

(a)	Purchases or sales of gilts by the Bank of England from or to UK banks	
(b)	Trading of zero-coupon bonds in the London financial markets	
(c)	Sales and purchases by UK banks of foreign currency deposits	
(d)	The issue of new equity shares by UK banks	

Select the **one** correct option.

5.3 Recession is a term used to describe a period during which:

(a)	Gross Domestic Product stays at the same level for two successive quarters	
(b)	Gross Domestic Product falls for two successive quarters	
(c)	The Bank of England imposes a limit on bank lending for two successive quarters	
(d)	Interest rates rise for two successive quarters	

Select the **one** correct option.

5.4   Banks must maintain liquidity so that they can:

(a)	Provide funds for the Bank of England	
(b)	Maintain an acceptable level of profitability	
(c)	Repay customer deposits if they are required to do so	

Select the **one** correct option.

5.5   The Bank of England helps to control the money supply through the Monetary Control Committee by:

(a)	Setting short-term interest rates	
(b)	Setting long-term interest rates	
(c)	Adjusting the UK Gold Reserves	

Select the **one** correct option.

5.6   A rise in interest rates in the UK economy will normally:

(a)	Increase business activity because more businesses will be able to borrow	
(b)	Decrease business activity because businesses will be less likely to borrow	
(c)	Have no effect at all on business activity	

Select the **one** correct option

6   Raising short-term and long-term finance

6.1   The main advantage to a customer of a bank overdraft is:

(a)	The customer only borrows what is needed	
(b)	The limit will vary on a daily basis	
(c)	No security is ever needed by the bank	

Select the **one** correct option.

6.2   A 'variable' interest rate on a bank business loan means that the rate:

(a)	Varies according to the amount left outstanding on the loan	
(b)	Varies according to the length of time left until final repayment	
(c)	Is based on the bank lending rate, which varies over time	

Select the **one** correct option.

6.3   A business borrowing by means of a bank overdraft can calculate the interest payable for cash budget purposes by:

(a)	Applying the interest rate chargeable by the bank to the projected average overdrawn balance for the period	
(b)	Applying the interest rate chargeable by the bank to the projected average daily balance for the period	
(c)	Using the figure for interest paid on the overdraft for the comparable period in the previous financial year	

Select the **one** correct option.

6.4   Southern Bank plc has offered to lend Britten Ltd £120,000 to be repaid over one year in 12 monthly instalments of £10,425 per month.

The flat rate of interest being charged is: [   ] %.

Enter the flat rate percentage in the box above.

Calculations should be to two decimal places.

6.5   Factoring and invoice discounting are similar services provided by specialist companies for their customers. But the two types of service are operated differently.

You are to link with lines the two boxes on the left with the correct service features in the boxes on the right.

	the company carries out the credit control of the customer
factoring	
	the customer carries out the credit control
	the customer issues the sales invoices
invoice discounting	
	the company issues the sales invoices

6.6   A bank loan with an interest rate which includes a maximum rate quoted in the facility letter is known as:

(a)	A bullet loan	
(b)	A fixed rate loan	
(c)	A capped rate loan	
(d)	A commercial loan	

Tick the **one** correct option.

6.7   Different forms of financing – from leasing to share issues – affect the gearing of a company in different ways.

You are to complete the table below, indicating with a tick in the correct column the effect of the individual types of financing on the gearing.

Type of financing	Effect on gearing		
	Increase	No change	Reduction
Lease			
Commercial mortgage			
Equity shares			
Preference shares			
Loan stock			

6.8   **You are to** enter each of the following words or phrases into the correct box:

guarantees   **fixed charge**   **floating charge**   **assets**

A lender will often require [   ] as security to cover its lending to

company customers. This can take the form of a [   ] for non-current

assets and a [   ] over current assets. Additionally, third party security

in the form of [   ] from the directors may be used as security.

6.9   A business wishes to borrow £275,000 and has a property valued at £687,500 which can be used as security. The loan to value percentage will be (tick the correct option):

(a)	25%	
(b)	40%	
(c)	400%	

6.10   A company wishes to take out a bank two year fixed rate loan of £200,000. The capital and interest will be repaid at the end of each year, the capital reducing by two equal instalments.

The following terms have been quoted:

Flat rate interest rate (interest paid annually)	5% p.a.
Arrangement fee (paid on drawdown)	1%

(a)   **You are to** calculate the total **cost of repayment** by completing the table set out below:

Year 1	Capital repaid	
	Interest at 5%	
	Arrangement fee	
	Total paid in Year 1	
Year 2	Capital repaid	
	Interest at 5%	
	Arrangement fee	
	Total paid in Year 2	
Total paid over 2 years		

(b)   The Annual Percentage Rate for the £200,000 loan is quoted by the bank as 9.8%. This is different from the flat rate of 5% quoted because:

(a)	The finance is repaid over two years	
(b)	The rate takes into account the fee and reducing loan balance	
(c)	Interest rates may change over the two years of the loan	

Tick the **one** correct option.

7 Investing surplus funds

7.1 A company Treasury Department has the option of investing £500,000. The highest interest rate is likely to be received from an investment that is (select the **one** correct option):

(a)	Low risk and for a longer period	
(b)	Higher risk and for a longer period	
(c)	Low risk and for a shorter period	

7.2 Gilt-edged stock (gilts) are certificates which are (select the **one** correct option):

(a)	Issued by the banks and given a guaranteed repayment amount	
(b)	Issued by the Government and given a return based on the sterling exchange rate	
(c)	Issued by the Government and therefore very low risk	

7.3 Indicate in the table below whether the types of investment listed in the left-hand column are suitable for a risk-averse investor or a risk-seeking investor.

Investments	Risk-averse	Risk-seeking
Land		
Company loan stock		
Bank deposit account		
Government stock		

7.4   **You are to** calculate the amount a Local Authority will need to invest for one year to earn £5,500 interest at a fixed interest rate of 2.5%. Enter the figure in the box below.

£ [   ]

7.5   **You are to** calculate the interest yield on 3.75% Treasury Stock with a market price of £1.11p per £1 of stock. Enter the figure in the box below. Calculate to two decimal places.

[   ] %

7.6   **You are to** calculate the gross return in interest from the following investment accounts. (Ignore any compounding of interest.) Enter each figure in the appropriate box.

(a)   £15,000 invested for two years at 3.5%, a rate which includes a first year bonus of 1%.

£ [   ]

(b)   £10,000 invested in a 4% fixed rate five-year bond which has been cashed in after four years incurring a 2% penalty for early encashment.

£ [   ]

7.7   The running of a company Treasury should be regulated by a set of Policies and Procedures, which will ensure that the company's surplus funds are invested in a way that minimises risk.

Indicate with a tick which **three** of the following requirements are likely to be found in the company regulations:

(a)	Investment limits for various levels of employees and managers	
(b)	The permissible types of investment	
(c)	A minimum requirement for very liquid funds, eg 7 days or less	
(d)	Bank of England permission to invest in Treasury Bills and gilts	

7.8 Gerrard Limited has received £800,000 from the sale of a warehouse. The Finance Manager has researched options for investing the money over various periods of time up to five years. He has been advised to identify a low risk fund. He has shortlisted three schemes:

1 **Deposit account from Helicon Bank** (an unknown overseas bank)
Interest   4.5% p.a.
Notice required   7 days
Minimum investment   £1,000

2 **Money market account with LFC Bank PLC** (a UK bank)
Interest   2.25%
Notice required   1 month
Minimum investment   £50,000

3 **A 5-year bond with LFC Bank PLC** (a UK bank)
Interest   3.75% fixed
Notice required   Repaid on maturity. 1% early repayment fee.
Minimum investment   £50,000

You are to:

(a) Calculate the annual interest receivable on each option, assuming the £800,000 is invested. Enter the figures in the table and tick the option you consider to be the most suitable.

Investment scheme	Return £	Best option
Deposit account with unknown overseas bank		
National Bank money market account		
National Bank five-year bond		

(b) The company has a business loan with LFC Bank which is costing 6% p.a. and there is £560,000 outstanding including interest. The Finance Director suggests that this loan be repaid in full and that the balance could be invested for at least five years in the best of the three schemes. He says that this will save money, but he wants to know how much.

Complete the following calculation table, assuming that the loan is to be repaid:

A	Amount of annual loan interest saved if the loan is repaid =	£
B	Annual interest from the amount remaining from the warehouse sale that could be invested if the loan is repaid =	£
C	A + B =	£
D	Amount of interest that could have been earned on the investment scheme if the loan is not repaid =	£
E	C – D (to give the figure for the money saved) =	£

Answers to chapter activities

1 Managing cash flows

1.1 **(a)**

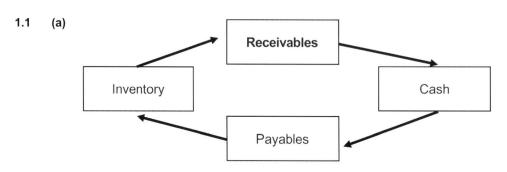

(b) (d) 70 days

1.2

Term	Meaning	Signs Include
Overtrading	Too little working capital	Rapidly increasing sales volumes Overdrawn bank balances Payments made late to suppliers
Overcapitalisation	Too much working capital	High cash balances Payments made to suppliers before they are due

1.3

(a)	Receipts that relate to the proceeds from the disposal of non-current assets are capital receipts	✔
(b)	Payments that relate to the acquisition of non-current assets are regular revenue payments	
(c)	Payments made to the owners of the business are capital receipts	
(d)	Income received from the operating activities of the business that is expected to occur frequently is a regular revenue receipt	✔
(e)	Income received from the operating activities of the business that is not expected to occur frequently is a regular revenue receipt	
(f)	Payments arising from the operating activities of the business that are expected to occur frequently are regular revenue payments	✔
(g)	Payments that relate to the acquisition of non-current assets are capital payments	✔
(h)	The receipt of a bank loan is an example of an exceptional receipt	✔

1.4   (c)   Overtrading

1.5

Example	Capital payment	Regular revenue payment	Payment for drawings	Exceptional payment
Dividends			✔	
Acquisition of new business				✔
Purchase of raw materials		✔		
Purchase of computer	✔			
Payment of Corporation Tax		✔		
Repayment of whole loan				✔

2 Forecasting data for cash budgets

2.1   (a)

	Sales volume (units)	Trend	Monthly variation (volume less trend)
August	56,160		
September	35,640	41,040	–5,400
October	31,320	42,120	–10,800
November	59,400	43,200	16,200
December	38,880		

The monthly sales volume trend is **1,080** units (the increase in the trend from one month to the next).

(b)

	Forecast trend	Variation	Forecast sales volume	Forecast sales £	Forecast purchases £
January	45,360	–10,800	34,560	172,800	103,680

Notes – The forecast trend is calculated by adjusting the last known trend by the monthly increase. The variation is the same as in October, as it repeats every three months.

2.2

	Selling Price £.p	Gross Profit £.p
Mark-up of 10%	214.50	19.50
Mark-up of 15%	224.25	29.25
Margin of 15%	229.41	34.41
Margin of 20%	243.75	48.75

2.3

20-3 Quarter	Trend working £	Trend £	Seasonal Variations £	Forecast Sales £
1	(43 x 550) + 78,500	102,150	−12,258	89,892
2	(44 x 550) + 78,500	102,700	+56,485	159,185
3	(45 x 550) + 78,500	103,250	+15,488	118,738
4	(46 x 550) + 78,500	103,800	−60,204	43,596

2.4 (d) £47.06

2.5 £2,249 *Workings:* £1,890 x 194/163

2.6 (a) See table on opposite page.

(b)

Year 14	Forecast trend	Seasonal variations	Forecast
Q1	1,920	+800	2,720
Q2	1,840	+320	2,160
Q3	1,760	−400	1,360
Q4	1,680	−720	960

2.7

Month	Jan	Feb	March	April	May	June
Price £	200.30	201.35	200.95	201.80	203.50	203.65
Index	100.00	100.52	100.32	100.75	101.60	101.67

2.6 **(a)**

Quarter	Sales units	4-point averages	Centred averages (trend)	Seasonal variations
Y10 Q1	4,000			
Q2	3,440			
		3,080		
Q3	2,640		3,040	−400
		3,000		
Q4	2,240		2,960	−720
		2,920		
Y11 Q1	3,680		2,880	+800
		2,840		
Q2	3,120		2,800	+320
		2,760		
Q3	2,320		2,720	−400
		2,680		
Q4	1,920		2,640	−720
		2,600		
Y12 Q1	3,360		2,560	+800
		2,520		
Q2	2,800		2,480	+320
		2,440		
Q3	2,000		2,400	−400
		2,360		
Q4	1,600		2,320	−720
		2,280		
Y13 Q1	3,040		2,240	+800
		2,200		
Q2	2,480		2,160	+320
		2,120		
Q3	1,680			
Q4	1,280			

3 Preparing cash budgets

3.1 **(a)**

	£	Workings £
Sales receipts	128,260	128,900 + 1,200 – 1,840
Purchases payments	51,330	50,060 + 8,900 – 7,630
Wages paid	21,400	No adjustments
Rent paid	12,300	12,000 – 1,200 + 1,500
Shop expenses	5,330	5,350 + 190 – 210
Depreciation	0	Non cash item
Bank charges	300	350 – 50
Drawings	20,000	Per narrative
Net cash flow	17,600	

(b)

	£
Profit	39,240
Change in trade receivables	–640
Change in trade payables	–1,270
Change in accruals	70
Change in prepayments	–300
Adjustment for non-cash expenditure	500
Drawings paid	–20,000
Net cash flow	17,600

3.2

	April £	May £	June £
RECEIPTS			
Cash sales	8,800	9,180	10,480
Credit sales	53,085	53,520	64,852
Bank loan	52,800	0	0
Total receipts	114,685	62,700	75,332
PAYMENTS			
Purchases	−36,650	−37,005	−42,075
Wages	−18,800	−18,950	−18,450
Expenses	−10,350	−11,260	−13,260
Capital expenditure	0	−59,500	0
Bank loan capital repayment	0	−1,100	−1,100
Bank loan interest	0	−528	−528
Overdraft interest	0	0	−300
Total payments	−65,800	−128,343	−75,713
Net cash flow	48,885	−65,643	−381
Opening bank balance	1,750	50,635	−15,008
Closing bank balance	50,635	−15,008	−15,389

3.3 (a)

	Actual sales £		Forecast sales £			
	January	February	March	April	May	June
Total sales	18,500	19,600	19,100	22,000	21,600	23,400
Cash sales	5,550	5,880	5,730	6,600	6,480	7,020
Credit sales	12,950	13,720	13,370	15,400	15,120	16,380

(b)

	Credit sales £	Cash received February £	March £	April £	May £	June £
January	12,950	7,770	5,180			
February	13,720		8,232	5,488		
March	13,370			8,022	5,348	
April	15,400				9,240	6,160
May	15,120					9,072
Monthly credit sales receipts			13,412	13,510	14,588	15,232

3.4

	October £	November £	December £
PAYMENTS			
Purchases	49,530	52,000	55,250
Wages	8,800	8,700	8,950
Expenses	6,450	7,100	8,050
New machine	13,500	13,500	13,500
Total payments	78,280	81,300	85,750

3.5

	Period 1 units	Period 2 units	Period 3 units	Period 4 units	Period 5 units
Raw materials usage	5,650	7,480	4,890	4,850	6,990
– opening inventory	1,070	1,200	1,375	1,080	1,500
+ closing inventory	1,200	1,375	1,080	1,500	Not known
= raw materials purchases	5,780	7,655	4,595	5,270	

	Payments in Periods:				
	Total £	Period 2 £	Period 3 £	Period 4 £	Period 5 £
Period 1 purchases	231,200	138,720	69,360	23,120	0
Period 2 purchases	306,200	0	183,720	91,860	30,620
Period 3 purchases	183,800	0	0	110,280	55,140
Total purchase payments				253,080	225,260

Using cash budgets

4.1   **(a)**

	Period 1 £	Period 2 £	Period 3 £	Period 4 £	Period 5 £
Original value of forecast sales	63,000	61,500	66,000	67,500	69,000
Original timing of receipts			63,750	66,750	68,250
Revised value of forecast sales	56,700	55,350	59,400	60,750	62,100
Revised timing of receipts			56,835	58,995	60,885

(b)

	Period 3 £	Period 4 £	Period 5 £
Original timing of payments	31,200	30,800	32,000
Revised timing of payments	37,360	31,040	32,200

(c)

	Period 3 £	Period 4 £	Period 5 £
Changes in sales receipts	−6,915	−7,755	−7,365
Changes in purchase payments	−6,160	−240	−200
Net change	−13,075	−7,995	−7,565

4.2

	£
Budgeted closing bank balance	4,690
Shortfall in receipts from credit customers	−2,080
Shortfall in cash sales	−4,750
Increase in payments to credit suppliers	−8,250
Decrease in cash purchases	+1,050
Decrease in capital expenditure	+18,500
Decrease in wages and salaries	+300
Increase in general expenses	−2,964
Actual closing bank balance	6,496

4.3

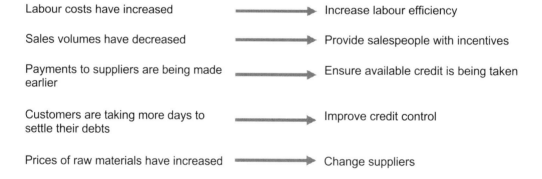

Labour costs have increased	→	Increase labour efficiency
Sales volumes have decreased	→	Provide salespeople with incentives
Payments to suppliers are being made earlier	→	Ensure available credit is being taken
Customers are taking more days to settle their debts	→	Improve credit control
Prices of raw materials have increased	→	Change suppliers

4.4 **(a)**

	Receipts from Sales in:				
	Month 1 £	**Month 2** £	**Month 3** £	**Month 4** £	**Total** £
Month 1 Sales	18,350	104,595	55,050		
Month 2 Sales		19,800	112,860	59,400	
Month 3 Sales			20,680	117,876	
Month 4 Sales				21,040	
Forecast Receipts	18,350	124,395	188,590	198,316	529,651

(b)

	Month 1	**Month 2**	**Month 3**	**Month 4**	**Net Total**
Change in Cash Flow	0	+49,545	−1,590	−3,564	+44,391

(c)   £798,700 x 60% x 5% = £23,961

5 The UK financial system and liquidity

5.1   (b)   Banks make short-term loans to each other

5.2   (a)   Purchases or sales of gilts by the Bank of England from or to UK banks

5.3   (b)   Gross Domestic Product falls for two successive quarters

5.4   (c)   Repay customer deposits if they are required to do so

5.5   (a)   Setting short-term interest rates

5.6   (b)   Decrease business activity because businesses will be less likely to borrow

6 Raising short-term and long-term finance

6.1 (a) The customer only borrows what is needed

6.2 (c) Is based on the bank lending rate, which varies over time

6.3 (a) Applying the interest rate chargeable by the bank to the projected average overdrawn balance for the period

6.4 The flat rate of interest being charged is: **4.25**%.

6.5

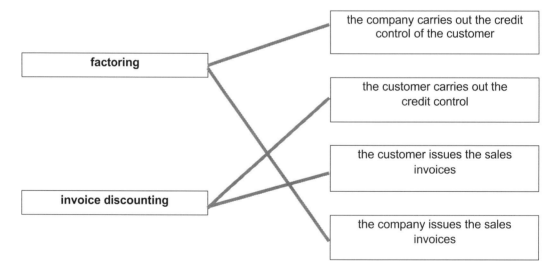

6.6 (c) A capped rate loan

6.7

Type of financing	Effect on gearing		
	Increase	**No change**	**Reduction**
Lease	✔		
Commercial mortgage	✔		
Equity shares			✔
Preference shares	✔		
Loan stock	✔		

6.8

A lender will often require ⎡ **assets** ⎤ as security to cover its lending to

company customers. This can take the form of a ⎡ **fixed charge** ⎤ for non-current

assets and a ⎡ **floating charge** ⎤ over current assets. Additionally, third party security

in the form of ⎡ **guarantees** ⎤ from the directors may be used as security.

6.9   (b)   40%

6.10   **(a)**

Year 1	Capital repaid	£100,000
	Interest at 5%	£10,000
	Arrangement fee	£2,000
	Total paid in Year 1	£112,000
Year 2	Capital repaid	£100,000
	Interest at 5%	£10,000
	Arrangement fee	Nil
	Total paid in Year 2	£110,000
Total paid over 2 years		£222,000

(b)   (b)   The rate takes into account the fee and reducing loan balance

7 Investing surplus funds

7.1 (b) Higher risk and for a longer period

7.2 (c) Issued by the Government and therefore very low risk

7.3

Investments	Risk-averse	Risk-seeking
Land		✔
Company loan stock		✔
Bank deposit account	✔	
Government stock	✔	

7.4 £220,000

7.5 3.38%

7.6 (a) £900 (ie £525 + £375)

(b) £1,400 (ie £1,600 – £200)

7.7 (a) Investment limits for various levels of employees and managers

(b) The permissible types of investment

(c) A minimum requirement for very liquid funds, eg 7 days or less

7.8 (a)

Investment scheme	Return £	Best option
Deposit account with unknown overseas bank	£36,000	
National Bank money market account	£18,000	
National Bank five-year bond	£30,000	✔*

*Helicon Bank's interest rate is higher but the risk is greater as the bank is overseas and unknown

(b)

A	Amount of annual loan interest saved if the loan is repaid =	£33,600
B	Annual interest from the amount remaining from the warehouse sale that could be invested if the loan is repaid =	£9,000
C	A + B =	£42,600
D	Amount of interest that could have been earned on the investment scheme if the loan is not repaid =	£30,000
E	C – D (to give the figure for the money saved) =	£12,600

Practice
assessment 1

Task 1

(a) Analyse the following activities into whether they will immediately increase cash, decrease cash, or have no immediate impact on cash.

	Increase cash	Decrease cash	No impact on cash
Write off irrecoverable debt			
Pay supplier in line with payment terms			
Revalue non-current asset			
Receive dividend from shares held as investment			

(b) A company had trade receivables at the start of the period of £45,860, and at the end of the period of £51,270. During the period a trade debt of £500 was written off. The credit sales during the period were £235,480.

Calculate the amount of receipts from customers in the period.

£ [ ]

(c) The following planned information is provided regarding the next year for a limited company.

Budgeted statement of profit or loss for year ended 31 December 20-5	£	£
Sales revenue		1,095,000
Less: cost of sales:		
Opening inventory	93,500	
Purchases	620,000	
Closing inventory	(105,000)	
		608,500
Gross profit		486,500
Expenses		292,500
Operating profit		194,000
Tax		66,900
Profit after tax		127,100

• Trade receivables are budgeted at £245,600 at the start of 20-5 and equal to 70 days' sales at the end of 20-5.

• Trade payables are budgeted to rise from £131,250 at the start of 20-5 to £139,800 at the end of 20-5.

• Non-current assets are to be used during 20-5 using an operating lease. The lease payments of £1,000 per month are included in 'expenses'.

• Depreciation included in 'expenses' is £22,100.

• Sale of non-current assets during the year is budgeted to raise £20,000 cash. The carrying value of these assets will be £17,300 at the start of the year. The profit on sale of these assets is offset within 'expenses'.

• Corporation tax liability is £52,200 at the start of 20-5 and budgeted to be £74,500 at the end of 20-5.

• The budgeted cash position at 1 January 20-5 is £101,500 overdrawn.

Required:

Complete the following table to arrive at the expected cash balance at 31 December 20-5.

Use + or – signs as appropriate.

	£
Operating profit	194,000
Change in inventory	
Change in trade receivables	
Change in trade payables	
Adjustment for non-cash items	
Purchase of non-current assets	
Proceeds from sale of non-current assets	
Payment of Corporation Tax	
Net change in cash position	
Budgeted cash position 1 Jan 20-5	–101,500
Budgeted cash position 31 Dec 20-5	

Task 2

Geebee Ltd is launching two new products in the next month, Exe and Wye.

(a)   Exe costs £76.00 to manufacture. The company is setting the sales price with a mark-up of 20% on cost price.

The sales price of Exe is £ [ ] .

(b)   Wye also costs £76.00 to manufacture. The company is setting the sales price with a margin of 20%.

The sales price of Wye is £ [ ] .

(c)   The sales volume of Exe in period 3 is forecast to be 19,500 using the regression line y = 15,000 + 1,500x (where x is the period).

The forecast sales volume of Exe in period 10 is [ ] units.

(d)   The company wants the sales revenue from Wye to be the same as from Exe in period 10.

The sales volume of Wye in period 10 would need to be [ ] units.

(e)   The cash budget for Whitesands Industries for the three months ended June has been partially completed. The following information is to be incorporated and the cash budget completed.

   •   A bank loan of £75,000 has been negotiated and this will be paid into the business bank account in April.

   •   The principal (capital) element of the bank loan (£75,000) is to be repaid in 60 equal monthly instalments beginning in May.

   •   The loan attracts 8% interest per annum calculated on the amount of the loan principal advanced in April. The annual interest charge is to be paid in equal monthly instalments beginning in May.

   •   When Whitesands Industries uses its bank overdraft facility, interest is payable monthly and is estimated at 2% of the previous month's overdraft balance. The interest is to be rounded to the nearest £.

   •   At 1 April the balance of the bank account was overdrawn by £1,350.

Using the additional information above, complete the cash budget (on the next page) for Whitesands Industries for the three months ending June. Cash inflows should be entered as positive figures and cash outflows as negative figures. Zeros must be entered where appropriate to achieve full marks.

	April £	May £	June £
RECEIPTS			
Cash sales	18,800	19,180	20,480
Credit sales	43,085	43,520	54,852
Bank loan		0	0
Total receipts			
PAYMENTS			
Purchases	−46,650	−47,005	−42,075
Wages	−18,800	−18,950	−18,450
Expenses	−10,350	−11,260	−13,260
Capital expenditure	0	−79,500	0
Bank loan capital repayment	0		
Bank loan interest	0		
Overdraft interest			
Total payments			
Net cash flow			
Opening bank balance			
Closing bank balance			

Task 3

A cash budget has been prepared for Princewood Ltd for the next five periods.

The budget was prepared based on the following sales volumes and a selling price of £4 per item.

	Period 1	Period 2	Period 3	Period 4	Period 5
Sales volume (items)	8,900	9,800	9,500	8,500	9,600

The pattern of cash receipts used in the budget assumed 50% of sales were received in the month of sale and the remaining 50% in the month following sale.

In the light of current economic trends, Princewood Ltd needs to adjust its cash budget to take account of the following:

* The selling price from period 1 will be reduced by 5% per item.

* The pattern of sales receipts changes to 20% of sales received in the month of sale, 60% in the month following sale and the remaining 20% two months after sale.

(a) Indicate in the following table whether the above adjustments are due to assumptions that are controllable or not controllable by Princewood Ltd.

	Controllable	Not controllable
Selling price reduction		
Change to sales receipts pattern		

(b) Use the table below to calculate the effect of the changes in the forecast amounts and timing of cash receipts for periods 3, 4 and 5:

	Period 1 £	Period 2 £	Period 3 £	Period 4 £	Period 5 £
Original value of forecast sales	35,600	39,200	38,000	34,000	38,400
Original timing of receipts			38,600	36,000	36,200
Revised value of forecast sales					
Revised timing of receipts					

Additional information:

The company's suppliers have negotiated reduced payment terms with Princewood Limited in return for fixing prices in the medium term. The original budget was prepared on the basis of paying suppliers in the month following purchase. The revised payment terms allow for settlement of 30% in the month of purchase with the remaining 70% payment in the month following purchase. These revised terms come into effect for purchases in period 1.

The original budgeted purchase figures were:

	Period 1 £	Period 2 £	Period 3 £	Period 4 £	Period 5 £
Purchases	21,500	21,200	20,800	22,600	23,000

(c) Use the table below to calculate the effect of the changes in the timing of purchase payments for periods 3, 4 and 5:

	Period 3 £	Period 4 £	Period 5 £
Original timing of payments			
Revised timing of payments			

(d) Using your calculations from parts (a) and (b), complete the table below to show the net effect of the changes to sales receipts and purchase payments for periods 3, 4 and 5:

	Period 3 £	Period 4 £	Period 5 £
Changes in sales receipts			
Changes in purchase payments			
Net change			

Task 4

(a)   An organisation has a policy of investigating all significant variances arising from the monthly cash flow budget, whether the variances are positive or negative. A new accounts assistant has suggested that a lot of time would be saved if only negative variances were investigated.

Briefly explain the advantages of investigating positive variances as well as negative variances.

(b)   The budgeted and actual cash flows for an organisation are summarised in the table below. A variance which is 6% or more of the original budget is deemed to be significant and needs to be investigated.

	Budget £	Actual £	Variance £	A / F
RECEIPTS				
Credit sales	453,600	420,530	33,070	A
Proceeds from sale of non-current assets	120,000	115,000	5,000	A
Total receipts	573,600	535,530		
PAYMENTS				
Purchases	151,200	140,850	10,350	F
Wages and salaries	144,680	154,000	9,320	A
Overheads	63,280	66,500	3,220	A
Capital expenditure	278,000	235,600	42,400	F
Total payments	637,160	596,950		
Net cash flow	–63,560	–61,420		

Identify each of the significant variances for the period. Explain for each of these variances how timing differences could be differentiated from more permanent variances. Provide possible reasons why the significant variances might have occurred.

Task 5

(a) A business has an average inventory holding period of 70 days. It receives payment from its customers in 96 days and pays its suppliers in 45 days.

What is the cash operating cycle in days for the business? (Select **one** option).

(a) 71 days	
(b) 121 days	
(c) 19 days	
(d) 211 days	

(b) Complete the following sentences by selecting the correct options:

Overcapitalisation can occur when a business has **[too much/insufficient]** working capital, and overtrading can occur when a business has **[too much/insufficient]** working capital.

Signs of overcapitalisation include **[high/low/normal]** inventory levels, **[high/low/normal]** cash levels, **[high/low/normal]** receivables levels, and suppliers being paid **[early/late/on time]**.

(c) The main aim of Monetary policy in the UK is:

(a) The maintenance of stable currency exchange rates	
(b) Maximising the supply of money in the economy	
(c) Keeping interest rates as low as possible at all times	
(d) Taking measures to control the supply of money in the economy	

Tick the **one** correct option.

(d)   Elder Limited has just received its end-of-year accounts.

Selected figures are shown in the table below.

	£000
Sales revenue	2,937
Cost of sales	876
Current assets	684
Current liabilities	663
Short-term debt (included in current liabilities)	115
Inventory	280
Trade receivables	395
Trade payables	162
Long-term debt	190
Equity	145

You are to calculate the following financial indicators and enter the figures in the boxes.

Periods of time should be calculated to the nearest day.

(1)   Trade receivables collection period =   days.

(2)   Trade payables payment period =   days.

(3)   Inventory holding period =   days.

(e)   Which **one** of the following would be the preference of a borrower when inflation and interest rates are falling?

(a)	A fixed interest rate on a loan	
(b)	A variable interest rate on a loan	
(c)	No preference	

(f)   If an investment has a low level of risk, what is the return likely to be?

(a)	High return	
(b)	Medium return	
(c)	Low return	

(g)   Rank the following assets according to their liquidity, with 1 representing very liquid.

		Ranking
(a)	Property	
(b)	Bank account	
(c)	Trade receivables	
(d)	Inventory	

(h)   Identify all of the following that are included within specific offences under the Bribery Act 2010.

(a)	Offering a bribe	
(b)	Bribing a foreign public official	
(c)	Agreeing to receive a bribe	
(d)	Bribing a UK public official	
(e)	Failing to prevent bribery on behalf of a commercial organisation	

Task 6

(a)   When interest rates are quoted for a loan, the Annual Percentage Rate will usually be:

(a)	Higher than the flat rate	
(b)	Lower than the flat rate	
(c)	The same as the flat rate	
(d)	The same as the simple rate	

Tick the **one** correct option.

(b)   NorthWest Bank plc has offered to lend Tippett Ltd £85,000 to be repaid over one year in 12 monthly instalments of £7,331.25 per month.

The flat rate of interest being charged is: [   ] %

Enter the flat rate percentage in the box above.

Calculations should be to one decimal place.

(c)   **You are to** enter each of the following words into the correct box within the text which follows.

capped   variable   interest   fixed   base

All bank finance is quoted with a specific type of [   ] rate. It can be

[   ] for the whole period of the loan, which means that budgeting will be

easier. It can alternatively be [   ] which is normally calculated at a

fixed percentage rate over the bank [   ] rate, or it can be

[   ] , in which case a maximum rate payable will be quoted.

(d)   A company wishes to take out a 10-year fixed rate loan of £80,000.

The following terms have been quoted:

- Interest rate (annual flat rate) 2.0% p.a.

- Arrangement fee (paid on drawdown) 1% flat payment in first year only

You are to calculate the cost of borrowing by completing the boxes set out below:

Total interest paid	£	
Arrangement fee	£	
Total cost of borrowing	£	

(e)   Tick the **two** features below which relate specifically to a floating charge as security.

(a)	It covers the non-current assets of a company	
(b)	It covers the non-current assets of a company or individual	
(c)	It covers the current assets of a company	
(d)	It can sometimes cover inventory which has been supplied but not paid for	

(f)   A company has agreed a bank overdraft of £50,000 on the following terms:

- The current annual interest rate is 18%.

- The interest is calculated on the closing monthly overdraft balance and should be included in the next month's opening balance.

- Assume that there are no differences in the monthly charges due to the number of days in each month.

Calculate the monthly interest cost (to the nearest penny) for each of the months shown in the following table. Use minus signs for overdraft balances and interest.

	Month 4 £	Month 5 £	Month 6 £	Month 7 £
Forecast net cash flow	−8,000.00	−4,200.00	5,150.00	−12,960.00
Opening bank balance	−9,600.00			
Closing balance before interest				
Overdraft interest to be charged				

Task 7

(a)   **You are to** calculate the gross return in interest from the following investment accounts. (Ignore any compounding of interest.) Enter each figure in the appropriate box.

(1)   £30,000 invested for four years at 4.00% p.a., a rate which includes a first six months' bonus of 1%.

£ [   ]

(2)   £12,000 invested in a 3% fixed rate two-year bond which has been cashed in after one year, incurring a 1.25% penalty for early encashment.

£ [   ]

(b)   Identify whether each of the following statements is true or false.

		True	False
(a)	Investing in gilts is generally low risk		
(b)	A balanced portfolio will normally reduce risk		
(c)	The skills of the treasury department are irrelevant when selecting investments		
(d)	The ethics of the business to be invested in is an important consideration for many corporate investors		

(c)   A company is considering purchasing 6% Treasury Stock with a redemption date of 2030. The stock is trading at £130 per £100 of stock.

Select the current interest yield (to two decimal places) from the following:

(a)	6.00%	
(b)	7.80%	
(c)	4.62%	
(d)	1.30%	

(d)   A company invested £25,000 in shares with a nominal value of 25p when they were trading at 50p per share. A dividend of five pence per share has been announced.

How much will the investing company receive in dividends?

£ [   ]

(e)   A company has invested £600,000 in a three-year bond paying 3.8% every year with interest compounding.

What will be the total to be redeemed at the end of the three years (to the nearest £)?

£ [   ]

(f)   Identify whether the following statement is true or false.

	True	False
Paper 'bearer bond' certificates carry a high security risk due to their easy conversion into cash		

(g)   A company is about to pay a dividend of £0.35 per share. The shares have a par value of £2.00 and are trading at £8.30.

What is the dividend yield (to two decimal places)? [   ] %

(h)   A company has invested £400,000 in a two-year bond paying 1.2% every six months. The interest is paid directly into the company bank account.

What will be the total interest received in the two years?

£ [   ]

Task 8

(a) Crescent Limited has a money market deposit of £400,000 which matures at the end of the month.

The Finance Director is interested in placing the funds in a long-term investment (up to 10 years), which provides an excellent return. Liquidity is not so important, as it is a long-term investment, but the Finance Director would not like to see the investment lose value over the long term.

The areas of investment that interest the Finance Director are:

• listed shares

• Government stock

• commercial property

You are to prepare briefing notes for the meeting covering the following aspects of each of the three forms of investment: risk, return and liquidity.

The briefing notes should be presented in 'bullet point' format.

(b) Greenpower Limited is a private company involved in the supply of components for wind turbines. In addition to family shareholders, the company is financed by a 'green partnership loan', which is part funded by the local authority.

The company has a policy on the investment of surplus funds that includes the following criteria:

- Investment in company shares must only be in companies that

    – have published details of how they plan to reduce their carbon footprint

    – are engaged in the production or sale of sustainable products

    – do not directly profit from the extraction or sale of fossil fuels

Suggest briefly the reasons why Greenpower Limited may have developed its investment policy with the restrictions outlined.

Practice assessment 2

Task 1

(a) Analyse the following activities into whether they will have an impact only on cash, only on profit, or on both cash and profit.

	Impact only on cash	Impact only on profit	Impact on both cash and profit
Sell non-current asset for carrying value			
Increase inventory level without using credit			
Increase provision for irrecoverable debts			
Pay quarterly VAT to HMRC			

(b) A company had trade payables at the start of the period of £25,660, and at the end of the period of £21,270. Credit purchases during the period were £144,410.

Calculate the amount of payments to suppliers in the period.

£ [   ]

(c) A company had a carrying value of non-current assets of £144,860 at the start of the period. By the end of the period this had risen to £151,500. Depreciation for the year was £12,680. A non-current asset was sold during the period for its carrying value of £1,200. Additional non-current assets were purchased for cash during the period.

Calculate the amount paid for additional non-current assets during the period.

£ [   ]

Task 2

(a) Create an index for the price of the commodity using month 1 as the base period. Round index figures to two decimal places.

Month	1	2	3	4
Price	£785.60	£799.45	£809.50	£793.80
Index				

(b) A company uses the least squares regression line to forecast sales. The regression line is identified as:

$y = 432{,}500 + 1{,}250x$

where y is the sales value and x is the month number. January 20-5 was month 20.

Calculate the forecast value of sales for June 20-5 using the regression line.

£ [   ]

(c) Assuming that each unit has a selling price of £250, the forecast sales volume for June 20-5 based

on the calculation in part (b) is [   ] units.

(d) The cost of manufacturing a certain product is £260.00.

Calculate the selling prices based on the following alternative assumptions:

	Selling price £.p
Mark up of 35%	
Margin of 45%	

(e) The cash budget for a company has been partially completed for two periods. The following information is to be incorporated and the cash budget completed.

- The company has £320,000 invested in a fixed term, fixed interest investment. Interest is earned at 0.25% per period, and credited to the bank on the first day of the period.

- The company plans to issue 200,000 ordinary shares with a nominal value of 50 pence each and a premium of 60 pence each in period 8.

- The company has agreed to acquire non-current assets through a finance lease in period 7. The assets are valued at £400,000, and require a deposit of 15% to be paid in period 7, followed by 60 instalments of £8,500 each commencing in period 8.

- Overdraft interest is payable at a rate of 0.5% per period based on the previous period's closing overdraft balance.

- The company needs to pay VAT in period 7 based on the previous quarter's data. All inputs and outputs are standard rated at 20%. The total inputs for the quarter were £1,200,500, and the total outputs were £1,395,600.

- The company must pay 25% of its estimated Corporation Tax liability of £350,000 in period 8.

- The balance on the bank account at the end of period 6 is expected to be £85,600 overdrawn.

Using the above information, complete the following cash budget for periods 7 and 8. Show cash outflows and negative balances with minus signs. Round to the nearest £.

Cash Budget	Period 7 £	Period 8 £
RECEIPTS:		
Receipts from sales	445,600	561,400
Proceeds from share issue		
Investment income		
Total receipts		
PAYMENTS:		
Purchases	−125,600	−87,450
Wages	−150,500	−147,360
Other operating expenses	−86,700	−93,570
Acquisition of non-current assets		
Payment of VAT		
Payment of Corporation Tax		
Bank overdraft interest		
Total payments		
Net cash flow		
Opening bank balance		
Closing bank balance		

Task 3

A company has forecast the following sales of a new product that will commence sales in Month 1:

	Month 1 £	Month 2 £	Month 3 £	Month 4 £	Total £
Forecast Sales	183,500	198,000	206,800	202,400	790,700

The expected receipts from sales are that:

- 20% are received in the month of sale (cash sales)
- 25% are received in the month following the sale
- 55% are received two months following the sale

This has produced the following initial forecast of receipts:

	Receipts from Sales in:				
	Month 1 £	Month 2 £	Month 3 £	Month 4 £	Total £
Forecast Receipts	36,700	85,475	191,785	201,080	515,040

The company is now considering offering a discount of 6% for credit customers who pay in the month following sale. This is expected to change the receipts profile to the following:

- 20% of sales are received in the month of sale (cash sales)
- 60% of sales are received in the month following the sale
- 20% of sales are received two months following the sale

All solutions should be shown to the nearest £ where appropriate.

(a)   Indicate in the following table whether the above adjustments are due to assumptions that are controllable or not controllable by the company.

	Controllable	Not controllable
Offer of discount for prompt payment		
Change to sales receipts profile		

(b)   Complete the following table to show the expected receipts if the settlement discount is offered.

	Receipts from Sales in:				
	Month 1 £	Month 2 £	Month 3 £	Month 4 £	Total £
Month 1 Sales					
Month 2 Sales					
Month 3 Sales					
Month 4 Sales					
Forecast Receipts					

(c)   Calculate the increased or reduced receipts in months 1 to 4 by completing the following table and using + or − signs.

	Month 1 £	Month 2 £	Month 3 £	Month 4 £	Net Total £
Change in Cash Flow					

(d)   Calculate the amount of discount that will be allowed on the sales made in months 1 to 4 based on the above assumptions.

£ [   ]

Task 4

(a) The budgeted and actual cash flows for an organisation are summarised in the table below. A deviation from the original budget which is 4% or more of the budget is deemed to be a significant variance and needs to be investigated.

	Budget £	Actual £	Variance £	A / F
RECEIPTS				
Sales	563,500	562,450	1,050	A
Proceeds from sale of non-current assets	29,400	22,000	7,400	A
Total Receipts	592,900	584,450		
PAYMENTS				
Purchases	165,500	174,600	9,100	A
Wages and salaries	180,600	179,950	650	F
Overheads	155,500	161,350	5,850	A
Capital expenditure	121,000	105,000	16,000	F
Overdraft interest	6,150	9,300	3,150	A
Total Payments	628,750	630,200		
Net Cash Flow	−35,850	−45,750		

Identify each of the significant variances for the period. Provide possible reasons why the significant variances might have occurred. Suggest corrective actions where appropriate and identify implications for future budget setting.

(b) Inventory is usually considered to be a less liquid form of current asset than trade receivables. However, some types of organisation typically have little or no trade receivables, and they may rely on their inventories to directly generate cash.

Explain why inventory is usually treated as less liquid than trade receivables. Suggest, with reasons, the type of organisation that this does not apply to, and that can use inventories to generate cash quickly.

Task 5

(a) If UK interest rates fall, the result is likely to be:

(a)	An increase in the cost of borrowing	
(b)	An increase in borrowing from banks	
(c)	An increase in the rate of inflation	
(d)	An increase in savings in bank and building society accounts	

Tick the **one** correct option.

(b) Wye Limited has the following extracts from its financial statements:

Statement of profit or loss		Statement of financial position	
	£		£
Revenue	650,500	Non-current assets	550,000
Cost of Sales	340,000	Current assets	180,500
Gross Profit	310,500	Total assets	730,500
Operating Profit	86,500	Equity	176,000
Finance costs	16,000	Non-current liabilities	280,000
Tax	12,500	Bank overdraft	103,000
Profit after tax	58,000	Other current liabilities	171,500

Calculate the following performance indicators, rounding to two decimal places:

Return on capital employed ⬚ %

Return on shareholders' funds ⬚ %

Operating profit margin ⬚ %

Gearing ⬚ %

Interest cover ⬚ times

(c) The following figures have been extracted from the financial statements of a company for the year
ended 31 December 20-5.

Statement of profit or loss (Extract) for the year ended 31 December 20-5	£
Sales	1,850,600
Cost of Sales	1,430,200

Statement of financial position (Extract) as at 31 December 20-5	£
Inventories	453,000
Trade receivables	508,900
Trade payables	435,250

Calculate the following (each to the nearest day):

	Days
Inventory holding period	
Trade receivables collection period	
Trade payables payment period	
Cash operating cycle	

(d) Which **one** of the following is a possible result of overtrading?

(a)	Having too much cash that is not being used effectively	
(b)	Being unable to meet liabilities due to shortage of cash	
(c)	Having to reduce selling prices to generate increased sales levels	

(e) If an investment has a high level of risk, what is the return likely to be?

(a)	High return	
(b)	Medium return	
(c)	Low return	

(f)   Which **one** of the following best describes a floating charge on a group of assets?

(a)	The assets are used as security for a loan and cannot normally be disposed of while the loan is still in existence	
(b)	The assets are used as security for a loan, but since they continually change, individual assets can be replaced in the normal course of business	
(c)	The assets are used as security for a loan, and some specified assets cannot be disposed of, but other individual assets may be replaced in the normal course of business	
(d)	The security for a loan takes the form of a document that states that if the borrower is unable to repay, then the obligation passes to another named party	

(g)   Identify all of the following that are included within specific offences under the Bribery Act 2010.

(a)	Promising a bribe	
(b)	Requesting a bribe	
(c)	Being offered a bribe	
(d)	Agreeing to receive a bribe	
(e)	Hoping for a bribe	

(h)   Identify whether the following statement is true or false.

Money laundering means exchanging money or assets that were obtained criminally for money or assets that don't have an obvious link to criminal activity.

TRUE / FALSE

Task 6

(a)   APR stands for:

(a)	Average Percentage Rate	
(b)	Annual Percentage Rate	
(c)	Approximate Percentage Rate	
(d)	Annual Preferred Rate	

Tick the **one** correct option.

(b)   Eastern Bank plc has offered to lend Barque Ltd £100,000 to be repaid over one year in 12 monthly instalments of £8,562.50 per month.

The flat rate of interest being charged is: [   ] %

Enter the flat rate percentage in the box above.

Calculations should be to two decimal places.

(c)   A company wishes to take out a one-year fixed rate 'bullet' loan of £100,000. The capital and interest will be repaid in full at the end of the year.

The following terms have been quoted:

Flat interest rate (annual)	2.0% p.a.
Annual percentage rate	3.0%
Arrangement fee (paid on drawdown)	1%

You are to calculate the **cost of borrowing** by completing the boxes set out below:

Total interest paid	£	
Arrangement fee	£	
Total cost of borrowing	£	

(d) **You are to** match the types of security in the boxes on the left with the correct descriptions in the boxes on the right. Draw lines between the boxes as appropriate.

commercial mortgage

a form signed by a Company Director promising to repay the debts of the company if required to do so

guarantee

a company pledging its current assets as security for company borrowing

floating charge

a loan for property secured on the property itself

(e) A company has agreed a bank overdraft of £60,000 on the following terms:

• The current annual interest rate is 21%.

• The interest is calculated on the closing monthly overdraft balance and should be included in the next month's opening balance.

• Assume that there are no differences in the monthly charges due to the number of days in each month.

Calculate the monthly interest cost (to the nearest penny) for each of the months shown on the following table. Use minus signs for overdraft balances and interest.

	Month 4 £	Month 5 £	Month 6 £	Month 7 £
Forecast net cash flow	−15,000.00	−9,200.00	12,480.00	−18,050.00
Opening bank balance	−19,200.00			
Closing balance before interest				
Overdraft interest to be charged				

Task 7

(a) You are to calculate the amount a business will need to invest for one year to earn £1,200 interest at a fixed interest rate of 2%. Enter the figure in the box below.

£ [   ]

(b) Your company's Treasury has a 12-month bond investment of £120,000 (including interest) which is maturing next week.

The company also has a £50,000 bank loan with the relatively high interest rate of 7%.

You are weighing up the possible choices for the use of these maturing funds. There are two favoured options:

(1) Reinvest the whole of the £120,000 in another one-year bond which pays an interest rate of 3.5%.

(2) Repay the borrowing of £50,000 and use the balance to invest in the same 3.5% bond scheme.

You are to complete the following table:

	£
Amount required to repay the loan	
Saving of loan interest payable over the following 12 months	
Amount which could be invested in the one-year bond after repaying the loan	
Annual interest receivable on option (1) above	
Annual interest receivable on option (2) above	
Financial gain in repaying loan and reinvesting balance	

(c) A company is considering purchasing 1.5% stock with a redemption date of 2030. The stock is trading at £95 per £100 of stock.

Select the current interest yield (to two decimal places) from the following:

(a) 1.58%	
(b) 0.95%	
(c) 1.50%	
(d) 1.43%	

(d)   A company invested £75,000 in shares with a nominal value of 50p when they were trading at 25p per share. A dividend of three pence per share has been announced.

How much will the investing company receive in dividends?

£ [   ]

(e)   A company has invested £200,000 in a two-year bond paying 2.2% every year with interest compounding.

What will be the total to be redeemed at the end of the two years (to the nearest £)?

£ [   ]

(f)   Identify whether the following statement is true or false.

Investing in shares in a company that are valued in US dollars increases the risk because of future currency movements.

TRUE / FALSE

(g)   A company is about to pay a dividend of £0.18 per share. The shares have a par value of £0.50 and are trading at £4.30.

What is the dividend yield (to two decimal places)? [   ] %

(h)   A company has invested £700,000 in a two-year bond paying 0.2% every month. The interest is paid directly into the company bank account.

What will be the total interest received in the two years?

£ [   ]

Task 8

Mushtaq, Muswell & Hill Co, a small firm of solicitors, manages a portfolio of individual short-term deposits which represent its clients' funds. The value of this portfolio has increased considerably over the last twelve months.

Solicitors' regulations require that these funds are held as 'client accounts' in the form of deposit accounts at banks and building societies.

The Managing Partner is interested in consolidating a selected number of the bank deposit account funds operated by his firm to increase the return that can be made.

He has some questions to ask before making any decisions. These are:

1   'How will the return we make on the money be affected if:

  –   the amount deposited is larger?

  –   the period of the deposit is longer?

  –   the length of notice required for withdrawal is longer?'

2   'What difference does it make to the return if the amount is a fixed sum over a fixed period?'

3   'What are the implications if there are penalties payable if the money is withdrawn earlier than is stipulated in the account terms?'

4   'Are all banks and building societies safe for investing money? I have heard that the overseas Bank of Positania is offering good rates.'

(a)   You are to prepare a series of notes which explain the aspects of return, liquidity and risk as they relate to bank and building society deposits.

The briefing notes should be presented in 'bullet point' format.

(b) Suggest reasons why the solicitors' regulations require that clients' funds are held as 'client accounts' in the form of deposit accounts at banks and building societies.

Practice assessment 3

Task 1

(a)   A company had a carrying value of non-current assets of £186,240 at the start of the period. By the end of the period this had fallen to £181,150. Depreciation for the year was £18,430. A non-current asset was sold during the period for £8,500, incurring a loss of £1,550. Additional non-current assets were purchased for cash during the period.

Calculate the carrying value of the asset that was sold.

£ [   ]

Calculate the amount paid for additional non-current assets during the period.

£ [   ]

(b)   The following planned information is provided regarding the next year for a limited company.

Budgeted statement of profit or loss for year ended 31 December 20-6		
	£	£
Sales revenue		1,642,500
Less: cost of sales		
Opening inventory	133,500	
Purchases	820,000	
Closing inventory	(115,300)	
		838,200
Gross profit		804,300
Expenses		472,500
Operating profit		331,800
Tax		73,450
Profit after tax		258,350

- Trade receivables are budgeted at £295,600 at the start of 20-6 and equal to 63 days' sales at the end of 20-6.

- Trade payables are budgeted to rise from £211,250 at the start of 20-6 to £229,800 at the end of 20-6.

- The carrying value of non-current assets is budgeted to be £558,900 at the start of 20-6, and £601,300 at the end of the year. Depreciation during the year will be £55,600, and non-current assets with a carrying value of £15,500 will be disposed of for no proceeds. All additional non-current assets will be purchased for cash.

- Corporation tax liability is £83,200 at the start of 20-6 and budgeted to be £74,500 at the end of 20-6.

- The budgeted cash position at 1 January 20-6 is £145,100 overdrawn.

Required:

Complete the following table to arrive at the expected cash balance at 31 December 20-6.

Use + or – signs as appropriate.

	£
Operating profit	331,800
Change in inventory	
Change in trade receivables	
Change in trade payables	
Adjustment for non-cash items	
Purchase of non-current assets	
Proceeds from sale of non-current assets	
Payment of Corporation Tax	
Net change in cash position	
Budgeted cash position 1 Jan 20-6	–145,100
Budgeted cash position 31 Dec 20-6	

Task 2

Jumbo Limited is preparing its forecast sales and purchase information.

The sales value trend is to be identified using a 3-point moving average based on the actual monthly sales values for the current year.

(a) Complete the table below to calculate the monthly sales value trend and identify any monthly variations.

	Sales value £	Trend £
August	163,600	
September	189,200	
October	154,800	
November	167,200	
December	192,800	

The monthly sales value trend is £ [   ].

(b) The selling price per unit has been set at £25.

The monthly sales volume trend is [   ] units.

(c)   The company has identified the following regular monthly variations:

Month	Variation £
January	−15,600
February	−4,400
March	+20,000

Complete the following table to forecast sales for the January, February and March immediately following the months in the table in part (a).

	Trend £	Monthly Variation £	Forecast Sales Value £
January			
February			
March			

(d)   The direct labour used in a product currently costs £12.00 per hour. Each unit of the product takes 15 minutes of direct labour time to manufacture.

The labour force is to receive a 3% pay increase.

In future, the direct labour cost to manufacture 20,000 units will be £ [   ] .

(e)   The cash budget for Boileroom Industries Limited for the three months ended June has been partially completed. The following information is to be incorporated and the cash budget completed.

- An invitation to current shareholders to purchase additional shares is being prepared. This is expected to generate £125,000 cash during May. Legal costs of £11,000 in connection with the share issue need to be paid in April.

- The business is planning to purchase and install new production equipment and use a training company to train the staff in its use. Purchase costs of £100,000 will be incurred in April, and installation costs of £15,000 will need to be paid in May. The training cost of £12,000 will also need to be paid in May.

- When Boileroom Industries Limited uses its bank overdraft facility, interest is payable monthly and is estimated at 1.5% of the previous month's overdraft balance. The interest is to be rounded to the nearest £.

- At 1 April the balance of the bank account was overdrawn £10,500.

Using the additional information above, complete the cash budget for Boileroom Industries Limited for the three months ending June. Cash inflows should be entered as positive figures and cash outflows as negative figures. Zeros must be entered where appropriate.

	April £	May £	June £
RECEIPTS			
Cash sales	20,950	21,010	19,990
Credit sales	154,320	133,500	141,650
Share issue			
Total receipts			
PAYMENTS			
Purchases	−88,560	−93,480	−90,560
Wages	−52,450	−53,480	−52,570
Expenses	−31,050	−30,990	−32,690
Purchase & installation of Production equipment			
Training costs			
Legal costs re share issue			
Overdraft interest			
Total payments			
Net cash flow			
Opening bank balance			
Closing bank balance			

Task 3

A company has prepared a cash budget for the first five periods of trading of a new branch that is to be opened. Each period is 30 days.

Each product has a budgeted selling price of £50, and all sales are made on credit.

The original budget estimates have now been revised.

	Period 1	Period 2	Period 3	Period 4	Period 5
Original budgeted sales volume (units)	2,350	2,560	2,660	2,800	3,000
Revised budgeted sales volume (units)	2,180	2,400	2,510	2,720	2,860

The sales receipts pattern has been estimated as follows:

	30 days after sale	60 days after sale	90 days after sale
Original pattern	70%	30%	
Revised pattern	60%	20%	20%

The original receipts pattern assumed no irrecoverable debts, but the revised percentages are after deducting an allowance of 4% of sales for irrecoverable debts.

(a) Indicate in the following table whether the above adjustments are due to assumptions that are controllable or not controllable by the company.

	Controllable	Not controllable
Allowance for irrecoverable debts		
Changes to sales volumes		
Changes to sales receipts pattern		

(b) Complete the table below to show the revised sales values and revised timing of sales receipts.

	Period 1 £	Period 2 £	Period 3 £	Period 4 £
Original sales value	117,500	128,000	133,000	
Revised sales value				
Original timing of receipts		82,250	124,850	131,500
Revised timing of receipts				

Additional information:

The material cost for each product was budgeted at £20 per unit, with payment being made in the **month following purchase**.

The company has now negotiated a 10% discount provided payment is made in the **month of purchase**.

The company does not intend to maintain any inventory of materials or finished goods, and will therefore purchase materials in the month of sale.

(c)   Complete the table below to show the revised forecast amounts and timing of payments for purchases in periods 1 to 4. Assume that the discount is taken. Use minus signs to denote cash outflows.

	Period 1 £	Period 2 £	Period 3 £	Period 4 £
Payment for purchases				

(d)   Calculate the budgeted cash balance at the end of period 4, assuming that the branch commences period 1 with a cash receipt of £15,000 from the company head office. Assume that there were payments totalling £85,000 for labour and expenses in addition to the payments for materials. Use minus signs to denote outflows.

	Amount £
Receipt from head office	
Total receipts from sales	
Total payments for purchases	
Total payments for labour and expenses	
Closing cash balance	

Task 4

The quarterly budgeted and actual cash figures for an organisation are provided below.

	Budgeted £	Actual £
Receipts from credit customers	251,300	225,950
Cash sales	45,300	53,250
Payments to credit suppliers	−149,500	−151,400
Cash purchases	−12,320	−10,400
Capital expenditure	−32,950	−34,000
Wages and salaries	−41,230	−40,980
General expenses	−51,020	−58,990
Net cash flow	9,580	−16,570
Opening bank balance	−22,480	−22,480
Closing bank balance	−12,900	−39,050

Prepare a report for the Budget Committee based on the above figures. The report should include:

(a)   A reconciliation of the budgeted and actual cash flows for the quarter that commences with the budgeted closing bank balance and concludes with the actual closing bank balance.

(b)   A brief explanation of the reconciliation prepared under (a).

(c)   Identification of the one category of receipts or payments that has had the largest negative impact on the cash outcome, together with suggestions of possible reasons and actions that could be taken.

Report	
To: Budget Committee	From: Budget Accountant
Subject: Cash Budget Reconciliation	

Reconciliation

Explanation of Reconciliation

Major Negative Impact

Task 5

(a) Select which of the following statements regarding the cash cycle are true, and which are false.

Statement		True	False
(a)	If there is no inventory held, and the receivables days are equal to the payables days, the cash cycle will be zero		
(b)	If the payables days are greater than the receivables days, the cash cycle will always be negative		
(c)	Assuming no change in receivables days or inventory days, the greater the payables days, the longer the cash cycle		
(d)	Assuming no change in payables days or inventory days, the greater the receivables days, the longer the cash cycle		

(b) If the inventory holding period reduces by 13 days and the payables days increases by 10 days, what is the impact on the cash operating cycle?

(a)	increase by 3 days	
(b)	increase by 23 days	
(c)	reduce by 3 days	
(d)	reduce by 23 days	

(c) Identify whether each of the statements is a correct or incorrect indicator of possible overcapitalisation.

		Correct	Incorrect
(a)	Increased use of overdraft facility		
(b)	High levels of slow moving inventory		
(c)	Payments made to suppliers before due		
(d)	High levels of receivables with ineffective credit control		
(e)	High cash and bank balances		

(d) Andreij Davisovich Limited has just received its end-of-year accounts.

Selected figures are shown in the table below.

	£000
Sales revenue	1,750
Cost of sales	896
Current assets	720
Current liabilities	680
Short-term debt (included in current liabilities)	120
Inventory	200
Trade receivables	388
Trade payables	258
Long-term debt	121
Equity	125

You are to calculate the following financial indicators and enter the figures in the boxes on the right.

Periods of time should be calculated to the nearest day. Other indicators should be calculated to two decimal places.

(1)   Trade payables payment period [   ] days

(2)   Trade receivables collection period [   ] days

(3)   Inventory holding period [   ] days

(4)   Current ratio [   ] :1

(5)   Gearing [   ] %

(e)   Which **one** of the following is a possible result of overcapitalisation?

(a)	Issuing shares at more than par value	
(b)	Being unable to meet liabilities due to shortage of cash	
(c)	Having too much cash that is not being used effectively	

(f)   Which **one** of the following best describes a fixed charge on a group of assets?

(a)	The assets are used as security for a loan and cannot normally be disposed of while the loan is still in existence	
(b)	The assets are used as security for a loan, but since they continually change, individual assets can be replaced in the normal course of business	
(c)	The assets are used as security for a loan, and some specified assets cannot be disposed of, but other individual assets may be replaced in the normal course of business	
(d)	The security for a loan takes the form of a document that states that if the borrower is unable to repay, then the obligation passes to another named party	

(g)   Identify which **one** of the following relates to which people and/or organisations the Financial Services Compensation Scheme can sometimes assist.

(a)	It covers private individuals only	
(b)	It covers private individuals and some small businesses	
(c)	It covers small businesses only	
(d)	It covers individuals, small businesses and limited companies	
(e)	It covers limited companies only	

(h)   Identify whether the following statement is true or false:

Money laundering legislation only applies to UK.

TRUE / FALSE

Task 6

(a)   APR stands for:

(a)	Absolute Percentage Rate	
(b)	Adequacy Performance Ratio	
(c)	Annual Percentage Rate	
(d)	Approximate Payback Rate	

Tick the **one** correct option.

(b)   Central Bank plc has offered to lend Mo's Art and Design Company £48,000 to be repaid over one year in four quarterly instalments of £12,540 per quarter.

The flat rate of interest being charged is: [   ] %

Enter the flat rate percentage in the box above.

Calculations should be to one decimal place.

(c)   A company wishes to take out a one year fixed rate 'bullet' loan of £50,000. The capital and interest will be repaid in full at the end of the year.

The following terms have been quoted:

Interest rate (annual flat rate)   3.5% p.a.

Arrangement fee (paid on drawdown)   1.25%

You are to calculate the total **cost of borrowing** by completing the boxes set out below:

Total interest paid	£	
Arrangement fee	£	
Total cost of borrowing	£	

(d) A business wishes to borrow £350,000 and has a property valued at £700,000 which can be used as security. The loan to value percentage will be:

(a) 15%	
(b) 20%	
(c) 50%	

Tick the **one** correct option.

(e) A company has agreed a bank overdraft of £45,000 on the following terms:

- The current annual interest rate is 15%.

- The interest is calculated on the closing monthly overdraft balance and should be included in the next month's opening balance.

- Assume that there are no differences in the monthly charges due to the number of days in each month.

Calculate the monthly interest cost (to the nearest penny) for each of the months shown on the following table. Use minus signs for overdraft balances and interest.

	Month 4 £	Month 5 £	Month 6 £	Month 7 £
Forecast net cash flow	−10,080.00	9,200.00	−11,460.00	−11,090.00
Opening bank balance	−19,450.00			
Closing balance before interest				
Overdraft interest to be charged				

Task 7

(a)   **You are to** calculate the amount a business will need to invest for one year to earn £2,400 interest at a fixed interest rate of 3%. Enter the figure in the box below.

£ [   ]

(b)   Ilex Limited has a six month money market deposit of £150,000 (including interest) maturing next week. It would be possible to reinvest some or all of the funds at 2.5% p.a. (minimum deposit £50,000).

The company also has a bank loan with an annual interest rate of 8% and a balance outstanding of £60,000. Repayment is due in 12 months. The Finance Director has suggested that part of the maturing deposit could be used to repay the loan in full, but only if it would save the company money.

You are to complete the following calculation table (amounts in £s):

	Amount of annual interest on the loan that could be saved by early repayment	
plus	Amount of interest on reinvested money market deposit assuming the loan is repaid	
minus	Annual interest payable on the money market account if the loan had not been repaid and the money market funds had been reinvested in full	
equals	Financial benefit of repaying the loan from the maturing money market deposit	

(c)   A company is considering purchasing 2.5% undated stock. The stock is trading at £115 per £100 of stock.

What is the current interest yield (to two decimal places)?

[   ] %

(d)   A company invested £175,000 in shares with a nominal value of 100p when they were trading at 87.5p per share. A dividend of two pence per share has been announced.

How much will the investing company receive in dividends?

£ [   ]

(e)   A company has invested £600,000 in a two-year bond paying 2.6% every year with interest compounding.

What will be the total to be redeemed at the end of the two years (to the nearest £)?

£ [   ]

(f) Identify whether the following statement is true or false.

Investing in shares in a company operating in a country that has few restrictions on the use of child labour could have ethical issues for the investor.

TRUE / FALSE

(g) A company is about to pay a dividend of £0.16 per share. The shares have a par value of £0.50, were originally issued at a premium of £0.30 and are currently trading at £3.30.

What is the dividend yield (to two decimal places)?   %

(h) A company has invested £700,000 in a four-year bond paying 0.18% every month. The interest is paid directly into the company bank account.

What will be the total interest received in the four years?

£

Task 8

Prospero plc is a large travel company which specialises in arranging luxury island holidays.

The company runs a Treasury as part of its Finance Department. It has a strict investment policy established in a set of Policies and Procedures. These establish the authorities and responsibilities given to its Treasury employees and the types of investment which are permissible.

The investment manual of the Treasury includes the following policy for investing short-term surplus funds:

• The risk level must be low.
• The investment must be convertible to cash within 60 days.
• The maximum amount to be invested in any one type of investment is £200,000.
• The interest rate must be at least 1.5% above bank base rate.
• No deposits should be placed with financial institutions outside the UK.

The Treasury is reviewing its investment options at the beginning of the month and has selected four options for £200,000 which it has immediately available for an investment over one month. Bank base rate is currently 1%.

Option 1 – Blackstone Technology Fund

The financial press is recommending investment in this managed fund which is based largely on Far Eastern technology companies. The fund is currently yielding 5.6% p.a. and offers a potentially high level of growth over the long term. The publicity material sent out by Blackstone contains the sentence suggesting a high level of risk: 'The value of these investments may fall as well as rise.' There is no upper limit on investment in the fund. Minimum investment is £1,000.

Option 2 – Mercia Bank plc money market account

This is a UK bank money market based low risk product. The minimum investment allowed is £100,000. There is no upper limit on investment. There is a choice of two accounts:

(a) a 'call account' (money can be withdrawn at any time) – interest at 2.125% p.a.

(b) a one month fixed deposit – interest 2.5% p.a.

Option 3 – National Bank one-year bond

Investment in a reputable UK bank (low risk); projected interest rate is 4% and a minimum investment of £500,000 is required; one-year fixed period.

Option 4 – RWF Eurobank currency deposit

RWF Eurobank is offering good rates on Euro deposits, including a six month deposit paying 4% on amounts of €100,000 (approximately £85,000) or more. The risk of this investment is low.

You are to:

(a)   Complete the table below for each of the four options, writing 'yes' if the investment meets Treasury policy requirements and 'no' if it does not.

	Convertible to cash within 60 days?	Available for investment of £200,000?	Interest rate at least 1.5% above base rate?	UK financial institution?	Risk level low?
Option 1					
Option 2 (a)					
Option 2 (b)					
Option 3					
Option 4					

(b)   Write the text of an email to Miranda Smith, the company Treasurer, stating which of the four options should be chosen for the £200,000 available for investment.

Your email should state reasons for your recommendation. These reasons should be related to the factors of risk, reward and liquidity.

(c) Helios Limited is a rapidly expanding manufacturer of electronic scanning equipment. It is very profitable, financially sound and has highly experienced directors. It has recently been given a Government award for enterprise and innovation.

At a recent meeting of the directors there was a long discussion about the way in which some of the company's customers were exceeding their trading terms by purchasing beyond their credit limit and by paying their accounts late. The credit control section of the company, although it is well run, has become overstretched recently and this has contributed to these problems.

The liquidity of the company has consequently been under pressure, resulting in excesses over the bank overdraft limit (£150,000).

The Finance Director has asked you to prepare briefing notes to cover two possible financing solutions:

- an increase in the overdraft limit from £150,000 to £200,000

- factoring services from a finance company owned by the bank

The notes should be presented in 'bullet point' format and should include:

1 The main features of the two forms of financing

2 The advantages and disadvantages of the two forms of financing

3 A recommendation, with reasons, for the choice of one of the options

1   The main features of the two forms of financing:

2   The advantages and disadvantages of the two forms of financing:

3   A recommendation, with reasons, for the choice of one of the options:

Answers to practice assessment 1

Task 1

(a)

	Increase cash	Decrease cash	No impact on cash
Write off irrecoverable debt			✔
Pay supplier in line with payment terms		✔	
Revalue non-current asset			✔
Receive dividend from shares held as investment	✔		

(b) £229,570 *Workings:* £45,860 + £235,480 − £500 − £51,270

(c)

	£
Operating profit	194,000
Change in inventory	−11,500
Change in trade receivables	+35,600
Change in trade payables	+8,550
Adjustment for non-cash items*	+19,400
Purchase of non-current assets	0
Proceeds from sale of non-current assets	+20,000
Payment of Corporation Tax**	−44,600
Net change in cash position	+221,450
Budgeted cash position 1 Jan 20-5	−101,500
Budgeted cash position 31 Dec 20-5	+119,950

Workings:

*Depreciation £22,100 − profit on disposal of non-current assets £2,700 = £19,400.

**Opening balance £52,200 + charge £66,900 − closing balance £74,500 = £44,600.

Task 2

(a) The sales price of Exe is **£91.20**.

(b) The sales price of Wye is **£95.00**.

(c) The forecast sales volume of Exe in period 10 is **30,000** units.

(d) The sales volume of Wye in period 10 would need to be **28,800** units.

(e)

	April £	May £	June £
RECEIPTS			
Cash sales	18,800	19,180	20,480
Credit sales	43,085	43,520	54,852
Bank loan	75,000	0	0
Total receipts	136,885	62,700	75,332
PAYMENTS			
Purchases	−46,650	−47,005	−42,075
Wages	−18,800	−18,950	−18,450
Expenses	−10,350	−11,260	−13,260
Capital expenditure	0	−79,500	0
Bank loan capital repayment	0	−1,250	−1,250
Bank loan interest	0	−500	−500
Overdraft interest	−27	0	−721
Total payments	−75,827	−158,465	76,256
Net cash flow	61,058	−95,765	−924
Opening bank balance	−1,350	59,708	−36,057
Closing bank balance	59,708	−36,057	−36,981

Task 3

(a)

	Controllable	Not controllable
Selling price reduction	✔	
Change to sales receipts pattern		✔

(b)

	Period 1 £	Period 2 £	Period 3 £	Period 4 £	Period 5 £
Original value of forecast sales	35,600	39,200	38,000	34,000	38,400
Original timing of receipts			38,600	36,000	36,200
Revised value of forecast sales	33,820	37,240	36,100	32,300	36,480
Revised timing of receipts			36,328	35,568	33,896

(c)

	Period 3 £	Period 4 £	Period 5 £
Original timing of payments	21,200	20,800	22,600
Revised timing of payments	21,080	21,340	22,720

(d)

	Period 3 £	Period 4 £	Period 5 £
Changes in sales receipts	−2,272	−432	−2,304
Changes in purchase payments	+120	−540	−120
Net change	−2,152	−972	−2,424

Task 4

(a)

The reasons that all significant variances should be investigated and understood is so that any appropriate action can be taken. A positive variance in one month could be the result of a permanent change (for example increased sales), or a timing difference (for example earlier than expected receipts from sales).

If a positive variance is found to be permanent, then it could result in surplus funds that could be invested, or a reduction in a borrowing requirement. It could also indicate that the budget should be revised. If a positive variance is due to a timing difference, then it will have an impact on other periods. For example, sales receipts arriving earlier than planned may well result in a negative variance in the following period, and this must be anticipated.

(b)

Receipts from Credit Sales (7.3% adverse)

The information contained in the sales ledger control account should be examined to determine whether the actual sales in recent periods were below budget. If so, this would create a variance that could be permanent.

If the sales were in line with the budget then the adverse receipt variance must be due to timing differences. This could either be because trade receivables had increased (and the receipts should therefore flow in a later period), or because the amounts had already been received in an earlier period (ahead of budget). A further possibility is an unexpected increase in irrecoverable amounts, which would effectively turn a timing difference into a permanent variance.

Payments for Purchases (6.8% favourable)

The information contained in the purchase ledger control account should be examined to determine whether the actual purchases in recent periods were below budget. Purchases below budget could be caused by any of the following:

• reduction in prices

• running down of inventory

• reduced production

If the purchases are as planned, the variance could be caused by making payment in an earlier or later period. This could be evidenced by the levels of trade payables.

continued

Payment of Wages and Salaries (6.4% adverse)

Wages and salaries are normally paid with little or no lagging, so unless a budgeted bonus had been paid early or late it is likely that this variance is a permanent difference.

The variance could be caused by:

- more employees than budgeted and/or more hours worked
- an unplanned or higher than planned pay rise

Payment for Capital Expenditure (15.3% favourable)

The capital expenditure documentation (including approvals) should be examined to see whether the difference will be paid for later or is a genuine saving. Details of the cumulative capital amount spent would also be helpful.

The variance could be caused by a slippage in acquiring non-current assets, or difference in planned and actual cost (or a combination). It is also possible that a higher amount was spent in an earlier period and that this is a result of that situation.

Task 5

(a)   (b)   121 days

(b)   Overcapitalisation can occur when a business has **too much** working capital and overtrading can occur when a business has **insufficient** working capital.

Signs of overcapitalisation include **high** inventory levels, **high** cash levels, **high** receivables levels, and suppliers being paid **early**.

(c)   (d)   Taking measures to control the supply of money in the economy

(d)   (1)   Trade receivables collection period = **49** days.

(2)   Trade payables payment period = **67** days.

(3)   Inventory holding period = **117** days.

(e)   (b)   A variable interest rate on a loan

(f)   (c)   Low return

(g)   Ranking: **(a)** = 4; **(b)** = 1; **(c)** = 2; **(d)** = 3

(h)   (a), (b), (c) and (e)

Task 6

(a) (a) Higher than the flat rate

(b) The flat rate of interest being charged is: **3.5%**

(c) All bank finance is quoted with a specific type of **interest** rate. It can be **fixed** for the whole period of the loan, which means that budgeting will be easier.

It can alternatively be **variable** which is normally calculated at a fixed percentage rate over the bank **base** rate, or it can be **capped**, in which case a maximum rate payable will be quoted.

(d) Total interest paid £16,000

Arrangement fee £800

Total cost of borrowing £16,800

(e) (c) It covers the current assets of a company

(d) It can sometimes cover inventory which has been supplied but not paid for

(f)

	Month 4 £	Month 5 £	Month 6 £	Month 7 £
Forecast net cash flow	−8,000.00	−4,200.00	5,150.00	−12,960.00
Opening bank balance	−9,600.00	−17,864.00	−22,394.96	−17,503.63
Closing balance before interest	−17,600.00	−22,064.00	−17,244.96	−30,463.63
Overdraft interest to be charged	−264.00	−330.96	−258.67	−456.95

Task 7

(a) (1) £3,750 *Workings:* £600 + £450 [Year 1] + £2,700 [Years 2-4]

(2) £210 *Workings:* £360 − £150

(b) **(a)**, **(b)** and **(d)** are true; **(c)** is false.

(c) (c) 4.62% *Workings:* (£6.00 / £130.00) x 100

(d) £2,500 *Workings:* (£25,000 / £0.50) x £0.05

(e) £671,032 *Workings:* £600,000 x 1.038 x 1.038 x 1.038

(f) True

(g) 4.22%

(h) £19,200

Task 8

(a)   **LISTED SHARES**

Risk

- Shares have a recognised risk element, which will depend on the type of shares being purchased
- Share prices are subject to market fluctuations
- The investment could be lost if the company goes into liquidation
- Risk can be reduced by investing in a portfolio of shares with different risk profiles or in managed funds which invest in a wide range of shares in a particular area

Return

- Shares are often held for the long term as their value will generally increase in line with the stock market indices
- If shares are held for the short term, the return may be negative if they fall in value
- The cost of dealing in shares can be high and will need to be offset against the return received from capital gain and dividend income

Liquidity

- Shares can be sold at short notice to realise cash but this could result in a loss being made
- Shares are normally viewed as being a long-term investment

GOVERNMENT STOCK

Risk

- Risk is very low because the gilt-edged stock is issued on behalf of the Government and so carries a state-owned risk profile
- There is an economic risk if interest rates rise to a higher level than was expected by the market as this will reduce the value of the investment

Return

- The two indicators that need to be examined are:
  - the interest yield which relates the price paid for the stock to its stated interest rate
  - the redemption yield which takes into account the fall or rise in value of the stock as it reaches the redemption (repayment) date
- A rise in interest rates would cause the market price of the stock to fall, although the actual interest received by the existing holders of stock would be unaffected

Liquidity

- This stock is very liquid because it can be sold at any time
- This type of investment, however, is normally held for the long term because it is a very low risk investment

COMMERCIAL PROPERTY

Risk

- Commercial property has the advantage of being a physical asset which should always have value
- The value of commercial property has, however, been volatile in recent years, and with the changing face of retailing and office work it is likely to remain so

Return

- The return should be in the form of rental income. Provided the property is permanently tenanted on acceptable terms, this should provide an economic return

- There is a considerable risk of not finding or retaining tenants, which can reduce any return to zero, and still incur maintenance costs

Liquidity
- It can take a considerable time to sell a commercial property, so the investment is not liquid. If a sale is required because the building is untenanted, then this will become even more difficult

(b)

Reasons could include the following (which could be incorporated in company policy):
- The family shareholders may hold strong moral views about combatting the climate crisis
- The 'green partnership loan' may have stipulations that require such an investment policy
- The directors may wish to align the company's own products with other 'green' companies
- The directors may wish to build their 'green' brand, and avoid any adverse publicity or loss of reputation if investments were made in companies that did not align with their own ethical position

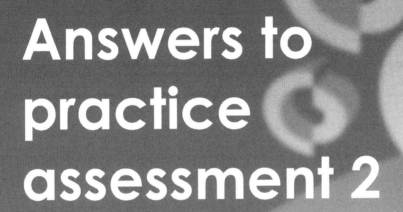

Answers to
practice
assessment 2

Task 1

(a)

	Impact only on cash	Impact only on profit	Impact on both cash and profit
Sell non-current asset for carrying value	✔		
Increase inventory level without using credit	✔		
Increase provision for irrecoverable debts		✔	
Pay quarterly VAT to HMRC	✔		

(b)   £148,800

(c)   £20,520

Task 2

(a)

Month	1	2	3	4
Price	£785.60	£799.45	£809.50	£793.80
Index		101.76	103.04	101.04

(b)   £463,750

(c)   1,855 units

(d)

	Selling price £.p
Mark-up of 35%	351.00
Margin of 45%	472.73

(e)

Cash Budget	Period 7 £	Period 8 £
RECEIPTS:		
Receipts from sales	445,600	561,400
Proceeds from share issue	0	220,000
Investment income	800	800
Total receipts	446,400	782,200
PAYMENTS:		
Purchases	−125,600	−87,450
Wages	−150,500	−147,360
Other operating expenses	−86,700	−93,570
Acquisition of non-current assets	−60,000	−8,500
Payment of VAT	−39,020	0
Payment of Corporation Tax	0	−87,500
Bank overdraft interest	−428	−507
Total payments	−462,248	−424,887
Net cash flow	−15,848	357,313
Opening bank balance	−85,600	−101,448
Closing bank balance	−101,448	255,865

Task 3

(a)

	Controllable	Not controllable
Offer of discount for prompt payment	✔	
Change to sales receipts profile		✔

(b)

	Receipts from Sales in:				
	Month 1 £	Month 2 £	Month 3 £	Month 4 £	Total £
Month 1 Sales	36,700	103,494	36,700		
Month 2 Sales		39,600	111,672	39,600	
Month 3 Sales			41,360	116,635	
Month 4 Sales				40,480	
Forecast Receipts	36,700	143,094	189,732	196,715	566,241

(c)

	Month 1 £	Month 2 £	Month 3 £	Month 4 £	Net Total £
Change in Cash Flow	+0	+57,619	−2,053	−4,365	+51,201

(d)   £28,465

Workings: £790,700 x 6% x 60%

Task 4

(a)

Proceeds from sale of non-current assets (25% adverse)

Possible reasons:

- Lower than expected proceeds from planned asset sales
- Fewer assets than expected sold (possible delayed sales, could be linked to capital expenditure variance)

Possible actions:

- If due to lower proceeds, obtain better forecasts in future
- If due to delays, plan for receipts to occur in future periods

Purchases (5.5% adverse)

Possible reasons:

- Increased purchase prices
- Increased production compared to budget
- Build up of raw material inventory levels compared to budget

Possible actions:

- Check prices of alternative suppliers and change suppliers if appropriate
- If production has increased, review future sales budget and update cash budget if appropriate
- Determine reason for build-up of inventory, and impact on future payments for purchases

Capital Expenditure (13% favourable)

Possible reasons:

- Assets cheaper than budgeted
- Fewer assets purchased
- Delay in purchasing assets (may be linked to proceeds of disposal above)

Possible actions:

- Determine reason and budget for any future payments if appropriate

Overdraft Interest (51% adverse)

Possible reasons:

- Increased overdraft level
- Increase in interest rate charged – could be due to individual circumstances or general economic situation and change in base rate

Possible actions:

- Examine all aspects of liquidity management to reduce need for overdraft
- Attempt to negotiate improved interest rate terms

(b)

Inventory is usually treated as less liquid than trade receivables, as for organisations that trade on credit, inventory is two stages away from generating cash. Firstly, the inventory has to be sold, and secondly the customer needs to pay, after the appropriate credit period.

Organisations that do not follow this process include the retail sector (for example supermarkets). These organisations typically carry out their sales on a cash basis, and therefore have few, if any, trade receivables. Their inventory is only one stage away from generating cash, since as soon as it is sold, the customer makes payment. Even payments made by the customer using a credit card will result in a virtually immediate cash receipt from the credit card company.

Task 5

(a)   (b)   An increase in borrowing from banks

(b)   Return on capital employed **18.97**%

Return on shareholders' funds **32.95**%

Operating profit margin **13.30**%

Gearing **61.40**%

Interest cover **5.41** times

(c)

	Days
Inventory holding period	116
Trade receivables collection period	100
Trade payables payment period	111
Cash operating cycle	105

(d)   (b)   Being unable to meet liabilities due to shortage of cash

(e)   (a)   High return

(f) (b) The assets are used as security for a loan, but since they continually change, individual assets can be replaced in the normal course of business

(g) (a), (b) and (d)

(h) TRUE

Task 6

(a) (b) Annual Percentage Rate

(b) The flat rate of interest being charged is: **2.75**%

(c)

Total interest paid	£2,000
Arrangement fee	£1,000
Total cost of borrowing	£3,000

(d)

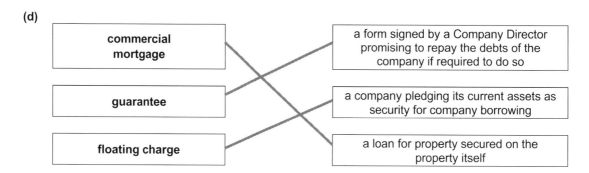

commercial mortgage		a form signed by a Company Director promising to repay the debts of the company if required to do so
guarantee		a company pledging its current assets as security for company borrowing
floating charge		a loan for property secured on the property itself

(e)

	Month 4 £	Month 5 £	Month 6 £	Month 7 £
Forecast net cash flow	−15,000.00	−9,200.00	12,480.00	−18,050.00
Opening bank balance	−19,200.00	−34,798.50	−44,768.47	−32,853.52
Closing balance before interest	−34,200.00	−43,998.50	−32,288.47	−50,903.52
Overdraft interest to be charged	−598.50	−769.97	−565.05	890.81

Task 7

(a)   £60,000

(b)

	£
Amount required to repay the loan	50,000
Saving of loan interest payable over the following 12 months	3,500
Amount which could be invested in the one-year bond after repaying the loan	70,000
Annual interest receivable on option 1	4,200
Annual interest receivable on option 2	2,450
Financial gain in repaying loan and reinvesting balance	1,750*

Workings: £5,950 (ie £3,500 interest saved + £2,450 interest received in Option 2) *minus* £4,200 (option 1 interest received) = £1,750 overall gain from repaying early

(c)   (a)   1.58% *Workings:* 100/95 x 1.5

(d)   £9,000

(e)   £208,897

(f)   TRUE

(g)   4.19%

(h)   £33,600

Task 8

(a) **1** **Factors affecting the return received on bank deposit accounts**

The following factors will normally affect the return received from the investment in a bank deposit account:

- The larger the deposit, the higher the return
- The longer the period, the higher the return
- The longer the length of notice required for a withdrawal from a deposit account, the higher the return
- The higher the risk, the higher the return

2 **Returns on fixed deposits**

- The deposit is less liquid and so the return will be higher
- It is important to match the maturity of the deposit to the date that the funds will be needed so that the return can be maximised

3 **The effect of early repayment of a fixed deposit**

- There is likely to be a penalty payable if the amount is withdrawn before the maturity date
- Any penalty will reduce the eventual return on the investment

4 **The risk factor of placing fixed deposits with a bank**

- A UK bank is normally seen as a low risk investment
- The UK Government is unlikely to allow a run on a bank
- The small business investor (turnover up to £6.5M) is protected by the Financial Services Compensation Scheme (FSCS), which guarantees repayment of deposits of up to £85,000 per institution in the event of a UK bank failure
- Relatively unknown overseas banks (such as the Bank of Positania) are normally considered as a high risk and are outside the UK Financial Services Compensation Scheme

(b)

Solicitors' regulations are designed to safeguard the funds that solicitors hold on behalf of clients.

By holding clients' funds separate from any other accounts that a solicitor may hold for his business, it avoids any mixing of money with the associated confusion over returns or possibly losses. It also prevents any possible illegal use of clients' funds, and it should reduce the possibility of fraud.

By holding such accounts only in deposit accounts in banks or building societies, this should help ensure that the risk of any investment is minimised (as discussed in part (a)). Bank deposit accounts are universally available to solicitors, and are a convenient way of investing, with access to funds tailored to requirements.

Answers to practice assessment 3

Task 1

(a) Carrying value of the asset that was sold: £**10,050**

Amount paid for additional non-current assets during the period: £**23,390**

(b)

	£
Operating profit	331,800
Change in inventory	+18,200
Change in trade receivables	+12,100
Change in trade payables	+18,550
Adjustment for non-cash items (1)	+71,100
Purchase of non-current assets (2)	−113,500
Proceeds from sale of non-current assets	+0
Payment of Corporation Tax (3)	−82,150
Net change in cash position	+256,100
Budgeted cash position 1 Jan 20-6	−145,100
Budgeted cash position 31 Dec 20-6	+111,000

Workings:

(1) Depreciation £55,600 + Loss on disposal of non-current assets £15,500 = £71,100

(2) Closing carrying value £601,300 – (Opening carrying value £558,900 – depreciation £55,600 – loss on disposals £15,500) = £113,500

(3) Opening balance £83,200 + charge £73,450 – closing balance £74,500 = £82,150

Task 2

(a)

	Sales value £	Trend £
August	163,600	
September	189,200	169,200
October	154,800	170,400
November	167,200	171,600
December	192,800	

The monthly sales value trend is **£1,200**.

(b) The monthly sales volume trend is **48** units.

(c)

	Trend £	Monthly Variation £	Forecast Sales Value £
January	174,000	−15,600	158,400
February	175,200	−4,400	170,800
March	176,400	+20,000	196,400

(d) In future, the direct labour cost to manufacture 20,000 units will be **£61,800.**

(e)

	April £	May £	June £
RECEIPTS			
Cash sales	20,950	21,010	19,990
Credit sales	154,320	133,500	141,650
Share issue	0	125,000	0
Total receipts	175,270	279,510	161,640
PAYMENTS			
Purchases	−88,560	−93,480	−90,560
Wages	−52,450	−53,480	−52,570
Expenses	−31,050	−30,990	−32,690
Purchase & installation of Production equipment	−100,000	−15,000	−0
Training costs	−0	−12,000	−0
Legal costs re share issue	−11,000	−0	−0
Overdraft interest	−158	−1,777	−685
Total payments	−283,218	−206,727	−176,505
Net cash flow	−107,948	72,783	−14,865
Opening bank balance	−10,500	−118,448	−45,665
Closing bank balance	−118,448	−45,665	−60,530

Task 3

(a)

	Controllable	Not controllable
Allowance for irrecoverable debts		✔
Changes to sales volumes		✔
Changes to sales receipts pattern		✔

(b)

	Period 1 £	Period 2 £	Period 3 £	Period 4 £
Original sales value	117,500	128,000	133,000	
Revised sales value	109,000	120,000	125,500	
Original timing of receipts		82,250	124,850	131,500
Revised timing of receipts		62,784	90,048	116,256

(c)

	Period 1 £	Period 2 £	Period 3 £	Period 4 £
Payment for purchases	39,240	43,200	45,180	48,960

(d)

	Amount £
Receipt from head office	15,000
Total receipts from sales	269,088
Total payments for purchases	−176,580
Total payments for labour and expenses	−85,000
Closing cash balance	22,508

Task 4 (a) to (c)

	Report		
To:	Budget Committee	From:	Budget Accountant
Subject:	Cash Budget Reconciliation		

Reconciliation

The following is a reconciliation of budgeted and actual cash flow for the quarter.

	£
Budgeted closing bank balance	−12,900
Shortfall in receipts from credit customers	−25,350
Surplus in cash sales	7,950
Increase in payments to credit suppliers	−1,900
Decrease in cash purchases	1,920
Increase in capital expenditure	−1,050
Decrease in wages and salaries	250
Increase in general expenses	−7,970
Actual closing bank balance	−39,050

Explanation of Reconciliation

The reconciliation demonstrates how each of the cash variances makes up the difference between the budgeted closing bank balance and the actual closing bank balance. The budgeted bank balance was £12,900 overdrawn. The difference between the budgeted and actual position for each category of receipt and payment is used to show how this budgeted bank balance developed into the actual bank balance of £39,050 overdrawn. The adverse variances are shown as negative figures here since they contribute to the deterioration in the closing bank balance.

Major Negative Impact

The largest negative impact is caused by the shortfall in receipts from credit customers. This could either have been caused by lower than planned sales, or by the inability to collect the receivable amounts in line with the budget.

Lower than planned sales could be caused by:

- a decrease in the volume of sales (for example fewer units being sold to existing customers, or a loss of some customers)

- a decrease in the prices charged

Improved marketing is one way to maintain sales in difficult trading conditions, but this is a complex area and decisions need to be made at a high level within the organisation.

If the sales are as expected, but customers are taking longer to pay than budgeted, then the issue is one of credit control. Rigorous procedures to chase customers need to be followed. Another possibility is to offer prompt payment discounts, although this has an impact on profit as well as cash flow.

Task 5

(a) (a) and (d) are true; (b) and (c) are false.

(b) (d) reduce by 23 days

(c) (a) is incorrect; the remainder are correct

(d) (1) Trade payables payment period **105** days

(2) Trade receivables collection period **81** days

(3) Inventory holding period **81** days

(4) Current ratio **1.06**:1

(5) Gearing **49.19**%

(e) (c) Having too much cash that is not being used effectively

(f) (a) The assets are used as security for a loan and cannot normally be disposed of while the loan is still in existence

(g) (b) It covers private individuals and some small businesses

(h) FALSE

Task 6

(a) (c) Annual Percentage Rate

(b) The flat rate of interest being charged is: **4.5**%

(c) Total interest paid   £1,750

Arrangement fee   £625

Total cost of borrowing   £2,375

(d) (c) 50%

(e)

	Month 4 £	Month 5 £	Month 6 £	Month 7 £
Forecast net cash flow	−10,080.00	9,200.00	−11,460.00	−11,090.00
Opening bank balance	−19,450.00	−29,899.13	−20,957.87	−32,823.09
Closing balance before interest	−29,530.00	−20,699.13	−32,417.87	−43,913.05
Overdraft interest to be charged	−369.13	−258.74	−405.22	−548.91

Task 7

(a)   £80,000

(b)

		Amount of annual interest on the loan that could be saved by early repayment.	£4,800
	plus	Amount of interest on reinvested money market deposit assuming loan is repaid.	£2,250
	minus	Annual interest payable on the money market account if the loan had not been repaid and the money market funds had been reinvested in full.	£3,750
	equals	Financial benefit of repaying the loan from the maturing money market deposit.	£3,300

(c)   2.17%

(d)   £4,000

(e)   £631,606

(f)   True

(g)   4.85%

(h)   £60,480

Task 8

(a)

	Convertible to cash within 60 days?	Available for investment of £200,000?	Interest rate at least 1.5% above base rate?	UK financial institution?	Risk level low?
Option 1	yes	yes	yes	no	no
Option 2 (a)	yes	yes	no	yes	yes
Option 2 (b)	yes	yes	yes	yes	yes
Option 3	no	no	yes	yes	yes
Option 4	no	yes	yes	no	yes

(b)   **Email text as follows:**

> Hello Miranda
>
> I recommend Option 2(b), the Mercia Bank one-month fixed money market account, as that is the only option that meets all our policy requirements. The reasons are as follows:
>
> 1   The risk level is low as Mercia Bank plc is a UK bank (not overseas) and the Government is very unlikely to let a UK bank become insolvent because this could cause a run on other banks.
>
> 2   The return on the call account is too low as it will only be 1.25% over base rate (it has to be at least 1.5% over base rate). The 2.5% return on the one-month fixed, however, matches our policy requirements, and that is the recommended choice. On maturity it is recommended that a similar investment is made as long as the interest rate remains at 1.5% above base rate.
>
> 3   The liquidity requirement of convertibility within 60 days is also met by the one-month fixed money market deposit.
>
> Regards
>
> A Student

(c)   **1**   **Features of an overdraft:**

- Interest is calculated on a daily basis
- Borrowing is up to a set limit
- Interest is only charged on the amount that is borrowed
- Interest is charged at an agreed rate, normally a fixed percentage above the bank's 'base' rate
- An arrangement fee based on a percentage of the limit is payable
- The limit is agreed for a set time period, often six or twelve months, but can be reviewed at any time to reflect activity on the current account
- Traditionally, overdrafts are repayable on demand but many overdrafts are committed overdrafts, ie only repayable on demand if the borrower becomes insolvent
- Security will be required for small and medium-sized businesses

Features of factoring:

- Factoring is the sale of the accounts receivable of a business for cash to a factoring company, which carries out the debt management and collects the debts when they are due
- A percentage of the value of invoices issued to customers (typically 85%) is paid into the bank account of the business within 24 hours
- The remainder is paid to the seller when the invoice is due, less the factoring company's charges

•   The factoring company takes on the debt management for the seller, including credit checks and debt chasing

2   Overdraft – advantages

•   It is flexible – the borrower only borrows what is needed

•   Interest is only paid on what is borrowed

•   The overdraft limit may be raised by the bank on request if the borrower needs extra working capital

Overdraft – disadvantages

•   It can be more expensive in terms of interest rates compared with fixed rate finance

•   It may be repayable on demand, but only if it is not a committed overdraft

•   Security may be required

Factoring – advantages

•   It turns unpaid invoices into immediately available working capital

•   It is an efficient debt collection service which helps to avoid irrecoverable debts

•   Debt insurance cover can also be arranged

Factoring – disadvantages

•   Costs

•   Some loss of contact with suppliers

•   Security may be required

3   Recommendation – factoring

•   The company needing the finance is expanding and financially sound

•   The liquidity problem lies with its credit control management

•   Increasing the overdraft limit will only be a short-term solution and will not address the main problem

•   The best solution appears to be the setting up of a factoring facility with a finance company which can run the credit control function

for your notes

for your notes

for your notes

for your notes

for your notes

for your notes

for your notes

for your notes